Basic Statistics Using Excel 2010

for

Basic Statistics for Business & Economics

Eighth Edition

Douglas A. Lind
Coastal Carolina University and The University of Toledo

William G. Marchal
The University of Toledo

Samuel A. Wathen
Coastal Carolina University

Prepared by

Ronald Merchant

Renee C. Goffinet-Meenach

Virginia E. Koehler

McGraw-Hill Irwin

Basic Statistics Using Excel 2010 for
BASIC STATISTICS FOR BUSINESS & ECONOMICS
Douglas A. Lind, William G. Marchal, and Samuel A. Wathen

Published by McGraw-Hill/Irwin, an imprint of The McGraw-Hill Companies, Inc., 1221 Avenue of the
Americas, New York, NY 10020. Copyright © 2013, 2011, 2008, 2005, 2002, 1999, 1996 by The McGraw-Hill Companies, Inc. All rights
reserved. Printed in the United States of America.

1 2 3 4 5 6 7 8 9 0 QDB/QDB 10 9 8 7 6 5 4 3 2

ISBN: 978-0-07-741682-9
MHID: 0-07-741682-1

www.mhhe.com

PREFACE

Basic Statistics Using Excel 2010 is a workbook, which empowers students to use the computer to help them understand and apply the basic tools taught in an introductory statistics course. When students use Excel to experiment and illustrate their problems, they can better visualize them and more easily see what happens.

Given the popularity of Excel and its continuing expanded capacity to handle statistical data, it is a natural in colleges; in fact, many colleges have Excel on all of their computers. In addition, Excel is the software of choice in today's business world. Since many students have already used this powerful software program and have it on their own computers what they learn with Excel can often be applied immediately on the job as well as in other classes.

This workbook is especially designed to accompany the Eighth Edition of **Basic Statistics for Business and Economics** by Lind, Marchal, and Wathen which uses Excel and Minitab illustrations. They sometimes use only Excel on problems where the authors feel Excel is superior and Minitab where they feel Minitab is superior. **This workbook fills a special niche for instructors who use only Excel 2010 in their courses**. It can also be used as a companion to most other introductory statistics texts, or by itself.

The chapter goals listed at the beginning of each chapter provides overviews of the main topics covered and the tasks students should be able to do after having worked through the chapter.

Following each chapter are several exercises to provide additional practice in applying the topics covered. Thus the students can check their comprehension of the material as they progress through each chapter. These exercises can also be used as class assignments.

The illustrations in this workbook are from Excel 2010 and are often different than previous versions of Excel. You may want to consider using a previous version of this workbook if you are using a previous version of Excel.

Ronald Merchant
Renee C. Goffinet-Meenach
Virginia E. Koehler

ACKNOWLEDGMENTS

We are grateful to many people for the help and encouragement throughout the development of this workbook: The people at McGraw-Hill Irwin, our students for their patience while classroom testing our rough drafts, and the feedback from several reviewers. Julie Sanborn's editing skills improved the earlier versions of this manuscript immensely.

We welcome comments about the book and suggestions for improvement:

Ron Merchant
4501 East Walnut Road
Gilbert, AZ 85297

rmerch8@gmail.com

CONTENTS

CHAPTER

1

USING MICROSOFT EXCEL SPREADSHEETS

CHAPTER GOALS

After completing this chapter, you will be able to:

1. Understand why Excel is so useful as a statistical tool.

2. Define what is meant by a spreadsheet.

3. Enter data into a spreadsheet.

4. Create formulas and solve problems with a worksheet.

5. Edit data that is in a spreadsheet.

6. Use a spreadsheet to experiment and illustrate.

Introduction

Welcome to **Basic Statistics Using Excel 2010**.

Excel is the most popular spreadsheet program in the world and has the capacity to handle a wide variety of statistical applications. Most colleges have Excel on their campus computers; it is part of the Microsoft Office package. You may have already had some exposure to Excel and used it for other applications. You may even have Excel on your home computer.

Using Excel will enhance your ability to understand and apply statistical principles. It is the software choice in the business world.

Basically, spreadsheets are used to help you with analysis of numerical data and to solve problems. In a spreadsheet, you can enter data that is related, and see what the results are if you change that data. You can create charts and graphs. You can run statistical analysis. Spreadsheets are used in businesses by managers to assist in decision making.

This chapter is for those who have never used a spreadsheet or worksheet, or for those who want a review of the basics.

Open Microsoft Excel. There are several rows across the top of your worksheet. The top row is the **Quick Access Toolbar**. In the upper left corner is the **Excel Button**. Next to it is a **Save** button and the **Undo** and **Redo** buttons. Using the pull down arrow, you can access a list of options that you wish to pin to the toolbar. It also shows the active file on which you are working.

The second row of your worksheet lists **tabs**. The middle row contains **command buttons** and the bottom row lists the **group names**.

As your mouse pointer rests on each button of the commands, a short description is displayed just below that button.

Creating a New Worksheet

If a blank worksheet does not appear, you will need to create a new worksheet.

To create a new worksheet, select the **File tab** located in the top left corner of your active window. From the pull down menu select **New**.

From the **Available Template** window, Select **Blank Worksheet**. Click on **Create**.

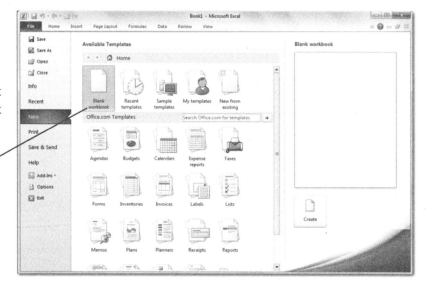

The worksheet consists of rows, columns and cells. Each individual rectangle is a *cell*. Each cell is identified by it placement in the Column (A, B, C ...) and the Row (1, 2, 3 ...). Thus, the cell B3 would be in the 2nd column and the 3rd row. The mouse pointer in Excel looks like an open plus sign. When the pointer is on a cell, click the left mouse button and that cell becomes the active cell. The cell will have a dark bordered box around it. You can also use the arrow keys: up, down, right, left, to move around in the worksheet.

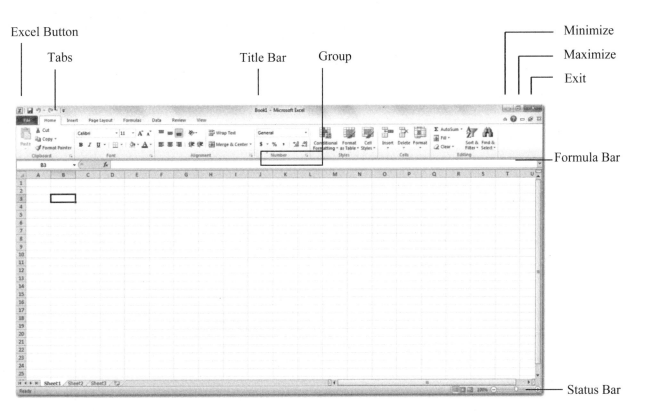

(Worksheet with cell B3 as active cell)

The data or information you key will show in the active cell and in the formula bar. When you press the <Enter> key, your data is entered into the cell and the cell immediately below becomes the active cell. Or you can point to another cell or use your arrow keys. To edit a cell, double click your mouse pointer in that cell, and the cell can be edited. The mouse pointer will show as a large I instead of an open plus. You may then edit the cell, without rekeying the entire contents.

You can select several cells at once to work with, called a range. A *range* is a rectangular group of cells. To use your mouse, you would place your mouse pointer on the upper left cell of the range to be highlighted, then click, hold and drag your mouse pointer to the lower right cell of the range, and then release the mouse button. The first cell shows a white background, all other cells in the selected range show a black background. A range is identified by its first and last cells with a colon in between.

1. Activate cell A1 by clicking on it, key **Schools** and press <Enter>.

2. Cell A2 should now be active. Key **Roads**. Key in the remaining data so that your worksheet looks like the one on the next page. Use the incorrect spelling of Supplie in cell A4.

If you make an error, you can correct it by immediately selecting the Undo button on the Quick Access Toolbar.

(Worksheet with range of cells B1:B4 selected)

To move text to a new position

1. Highlight the cells. From the Home tab, click on the Cut button from the Clipboard group.

2. Select the new location by activating the cell in which you wish the text to be located. From the Home tab, click on the Paste button from the Clipboard group.

If you wish to copy text, follow the same procedures for moving text, but instead of the Cut button, select the Copy button from the Clipboard group.

Excel allows you to check the spelling of the text in your entire workbook or just selected cells. However, worksheets are often created using abbreviations which this feature may not recognize. If this happens you can simply select Ignore.

1. To check the spelling of the whole workbook click on the Review tab. From the Proofing group select the Spelling button. A dialogue box will appear.

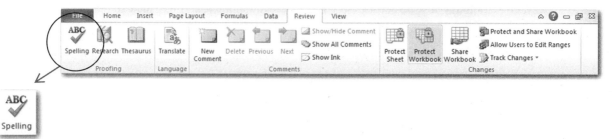

Depending on the cell that is active when you select the Spelling button, you may receive the following dialogue box. If you have not checked for spelling yet, then select Yes.

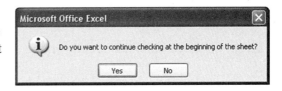

2. Click on **Supplies** and select <u>C</u>**hange**. Select **OK**.

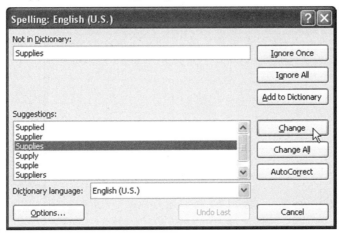

To check a selected area, highlight the cell or cells you want Excel to check, click on the **Spelling** button, and follow the same procedure as above.

You may create your worksheet in either portrait or landscape orientation by doing the following:

1. On the **Page Layout** tab, click the arrow at the right corner of the **Page Setup** group.

2. The **Page** tab should already be selected. You may select the radio button for **Por<u>t</u>rait** or **<u>L</u>andscape**. Select **OK**.

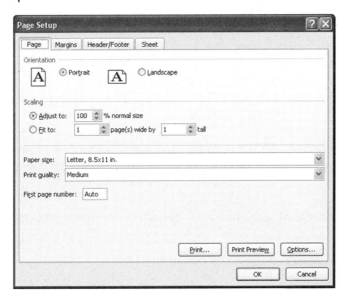

NOTE: As you work through this text, some illustrations may appear different than your screen.

Saving a Worksheet

To save a worksheet (file) do the following:

1. Select the File tab. Select Save As.

2. Key in the desired file name in the File name text box, key **Tax Dollars**.

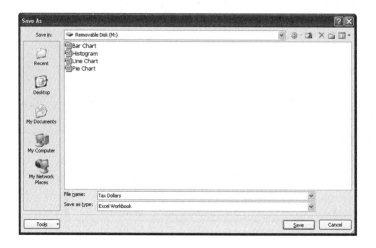

3. At the top of the dialog box, click on the down arrow at the right of the Save in: text box. Click your mouse on the location you want to save your file.

4. Click on Save.

Closing a Worksheet

To close a worksheet (file), do the following:

1. Select the File tab. Select Close. You may also click on the Close button at the far right of the Tabs row.

2. If no changes have been made since the last save, the file will close and the screen will be blank.

3. If the current information has not been saved you may select Yes to save the changes, select No if you do not want to save the changes, or select Cancel to go back to the current worksheet.

After you close a worksheet, you need to create a new worksheet or retrieve an existing worksheet to continue working.

Retrieving a Worksheet

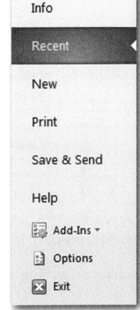

1. Select the File tab. Select <u>O</u>pen.

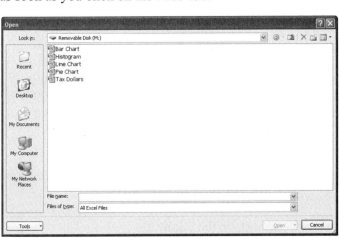

2. Verify the location of the file you wish to retrieve. You may have to change the selection in the Look in: text box at the top of the active window. The arrow to the right of the text box will allow you to access a pull down list of file location options. Recent files are also listed as soon as you click on the Files tab.

3. Highlight the file that you wish to retrieve by placing your mouse curser over the file name and click the left mouse button once.

If you do not see your file located in this folder, try selecting All Files from the Files of type: drop down list at the bottom of the dialogue box.

4. Once the file is highlighted, select <u>O</u>pen. Recent files are opened as soon as you click on them.

5. After making any changes, save and close the worksheet.

Using Excel to Solve Problems

Use a new worksheet to create formulas and solve problems. The following problem is an example of how one can use the worksheet.

We are interested in finding the percentage of change in the U.S. Department of Labor's projections of Fast-Growing Occupations in the United States from 2000 to 2010.

	Employment	
Occupation	2000	2010
Computer support specialists	506,000	996,000
Computer system analysts	431,000	689,000
Personal home-care aids	414,000	672,000
Computer software engineers	389,000	760,000
Medical assistants	329,000	516,000
Dental assistants	234,000	320,000
Social service assistants	271,000	418,000
Fitness/aerobics trainers	158,000	222,000
Medical records technicians	136,000	202,000
Database administrators	106,000	176,000

Source: U.S. Department of Labor

NOTE: As you enter information on the Excel worksheet, start **all** formulas with an = sign to distinguish a formula from text.

To enter this problem on your new worksheet, do the following.

1. Key the heading, **Occupation** in cell A1.

2. In cells A2 to A11, key in the occupations.

3. In cell A12, key in the word **Total**.

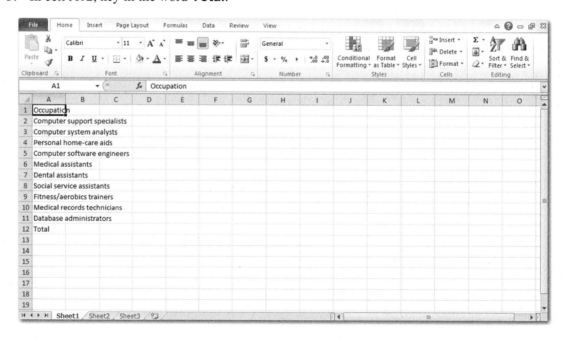

4. Notice that the names of the occupations extend into column B. To widen and automatically fit the column width, place the mouse pointer in the column headings row between columns A and B. The mouse pointer changes to a thick, black plus sign. Double click the left mouse button. The column automatically widens.

5. Key **2000** in cell B1 and **2010** in cell C1.

6. Fill in the amounts for 2000 in cells B2 to B11 and the amounts for 2010 in cells C2 to 11. Do not enter the commas as you enter the amounts.

7. There are a couple of different ways to sum several cells. Make cell B12 the active cell. Key **=sum(b2:b11)**. Touch the <Enter> key. The sum of the cells now shows in cell B12.

8. Now highlight cells, C2 to C11. To do so, put your mouse arrow on cell C2, click and drag down to cell C11. On the Home tab, in the Editing group, click on the AutoSum function button. Excel automatically enters the sum of the highlighted cells immediately below.

9. In cell D1 key **% change**.

10. Make cell D2 the active cell. Key the formula **=(c2-b2)/b2**. Touch the <Enter> key. The percent of change shows as a decimal number.

11. Make cell D2 the active cell. Put your mouse pointer on the lower right corner of the cell. It will show a small black box called a handle. The mouse pointer on the handle will show as a thick, black plus. Click your mouse button, hold and drag the mouse pointer down to cell D11.

Cells D3 to D11 have automatically been filled in with the formula.

	A	B	C	D	E
1	Occupation	2000	2010	% change	
2	Computer support specialists	506000	996000	0.968379	
3	Computer system analysis	431000	689000	0.598608	
4	Personal home-care aids	414000	672000	0.623188	
5	Computer software engineers	389000	760000	0.953728	
6	Medical assistants	329000	516000	0.568389	
7	Dental assistants	234000	320000	0.367521	
8	Social service assistants	271000	418000	0.542435	
9	Fitness/aerobics trainers	158000	222000	0.405063	
10	Medical records technicians	136000	202000	0.485294	
11	Database administrators	106000	176000	0.660377	
12	Total	2974000	4971000		
13					

12. Highlight cells D2 to D11. From the Home tab, in the Cells group, select Format. Select Format cells. Select the Number tab. Under the Category list box, select Percentage. In the Decimal places text box key **0** or click on the down arrow to display **0**. Click on OK. The amounts in column D now show as percentages instead of decimals.

Chapter 1

Sometimes you want to rearrange the columns. If you want to show a graph of the percents of change use columns A and D. To move the column D (% change) next to the column A (Occupation), do the following.

13. Click your mouse pointer anywhere in column B.

14. From the Home tab, in the Cells group, click on the down arrow next to Insert. Select Insert Sheet Columns.

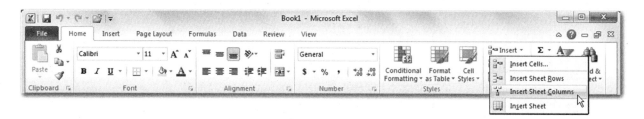

The information in columns B through D have been shifted to the right creating a blank column, with the width of column A.

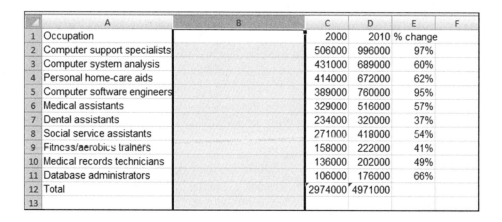

	A	B	C	D	E	F
1	Occupation		2000	2010	% change	
2	Computer support specialists		506000	996000	97%	
3	Computer system analysis		431000	689000	60%	
4	Personal home-care aids		414000	672000	62%	
5	Computer software engineers		389000	760000	95%	
6	Medical assistants		329000	516000	57%	
7	Dental assistants		234000	320000	37%	
8	Social service assistants		271000	418000	54%	
9	Fitness/aerobics trainers		158000	222000	41%	
10	Medical records technicians		136000	202000	49%	
11	Database administrators		106000	176000	66%	
12	Total		2974000	4971000		
13						

15. Highlight cells **E1 to E11**.

16. From Home tab in the Clipboard group, select Cut.

17. Make cell B1 your active cell. From Home tab in the Clipboard group select Paste.

The column with % change is now next to the Occupation column.

	A	B	C	D	E
1	Occupation	% change	2000	2010	
2	Computer support specialists	97%	506000	996000	
3	Computer system analysis	60%	431000	689000	
4	Personal home-care aids	62%	414000	672000	
5	Computer software engineers	95%	389000	760000	
6	Medical assistants	57%	329000	516000	
7	Dental assistants	37%	234000	320000	
8	Social service assistants	54%	271000	418000	
9	Fitness/aerobics trainers	41%	158000	222000	
10	Medical records technicians	49%	136000	202000	
11	Database administrators	66%	106000	176000	
12	Total		2974000	4971000	
13					

18. On the thick black plus sign between the column headings B and C, double click the left mouse button to resize the column width of B.

	A	B	C	D	E
1	Occupation	% change	2000	2010	
2	Computer support specialists	97%	506000	996000	
3	Computer system analysis	60%	431000	689000	
4	Personal home-care aids	62%	414000	672000	
5	Computer software engineers	95%	389000	760000	
6	Medical assistants	57%	329000	516000	
7	Dental assistants	37%	234000	320000	
8	Social service assistants	54%	271000	418000	
9	Fitness/aerobics trainers	41%	158000	222000	
10	Medical records technicians	49%	136000	202000	
11	Database administrators	66%	106000	176000	
12	Total		2974000	4971000	
13					

You can also select non-adjacent columns, simply highlight one of the columns, hold down the <Ctrl> key while highlighting another column. This can be done with as many as you wish.

Save your worksheet if you wish. Close your worksheet.

Exiting Excel

Select the File tab. Select Exit from the bottom of the menu. This ends your
Excel session.

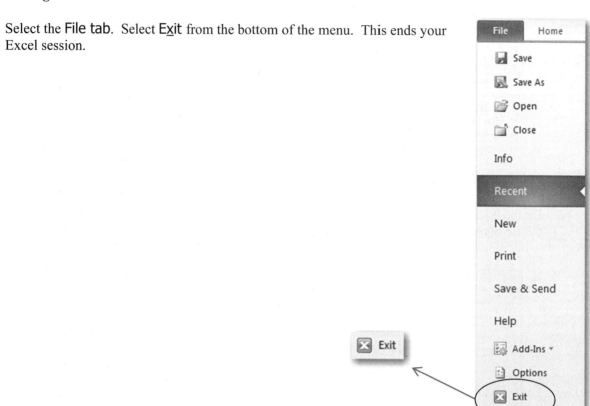

CHAPTER

2

DESCRIBING DATA: FREQUENCY DISTRIBUTIONS AND GRAPHIC PRESENTATIONS

CHAPTER GOALS

After completing this chapter, you will be able to:

1. Use Excel to create such common graphic presentations as pie charts, bar charts, simple histograms and line charts.

2. Edit and modify charts.

3. Print charts to be used alone or embedded in a report.

Introduction

The graphic presentations you see extensively in newspapers including *USA Today*, magazines and governmental reports often portray data from a frequency distribution in the form of pie charts, bar charts, histograms and line charts. Chapter 2 shows you how you can use Excel to create these charts and graphs.

Microsoft Excel's worksheets calculate and present differences and similarities between numbers, and changes in numbers over time. While these worksheets are useful they are often cumbersome to read. When you *illustrate* the data graphically it is often easier for your message to be understood. Sometimes a picture is worth a thousand words. With charts, you can make your data visual. You can create a chart to show the changes in your data over time, or how the parts of your data fit together as a whole. You can rearrange your data, even after you have charted it, or added additional data. With Microsoft Excel and the **Chart** group, you can easily turn your data into dynamic graphic presentations.

Pie charts show the relationship of parts to a whole. Bar charts show comparison between items or comparison over time. Line charts are often best for showing the amount of change in values over time. As you use different types of graphic presentations you will get to know which chart is best for your data. Since it is so easy you may want to experiment with several types of charts to see which chart does the best job of clarifying your point.

To create a chart on a worksheet, you will select the data that you want to use in the chart, and then use the **Chart** group from the **Insert** tab. The following exercises will take you step by step though the creation of several charts.

Pie Charts and Bar Charts

Example 1. The Clayton County Commissioners want to design a chart to show the taxpayers attending the forthcoming meeting what happens to their tax dollars. The total amount of taxes collected is $2 million. Expenditures were: $440,000 for schools, $1,160,000 for roads, $320,000 for administration, and $80,000 for supplies.

The instructions for entering the data and creating a pie chart are as follows:

If you saved the data Tax Dollars in Chapter 1, open the file and proceed with step 3. Otherwise do the following.

1. On a new worksheet, enter in cells A1:A4, the expenditure headings: **Schools, Roads, Admin** and **Supplies**.

NOTE: It is very important that all headings fit in **one** column. Either abbreviate the headings or widen the column to accommodate the length of the widest one.

2. Enter in cells B1:B4, the expenditure amounts: **440000, 1160000, 320000** and **80000**.

3. Position the mouse on cell A1, hold the left mouse button and drag until cells A1:B4 are highlighted.

As mentioned in Chapter 1, the first cell shows a white background and all other cells in the selected range show a black background.

4. From the Insert tab, in the Charts group, select Pie.

5. Several Chart sub-types are displayed. Choose the 1st one in the upper left corner. Be sure to have the chart selected.

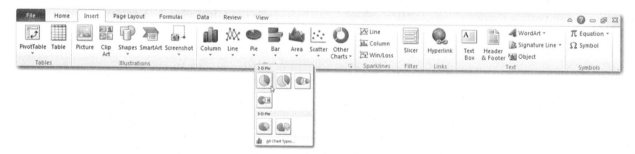

6. With the chart selected, a new set of tabs appears. From the Design tab, in the Chart Layouts group, click on Layout 1.

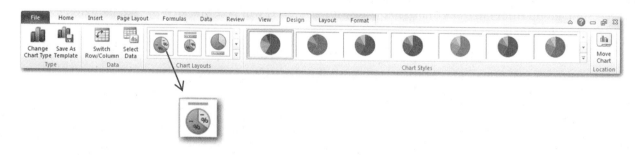

7. In your chart, click on **Chart Title**. A box appears around it. Key **Tax Dollar Expenditures**. As you type, the title shows in the equation box. Push **<Enter>**. The title is displayed in the chart.

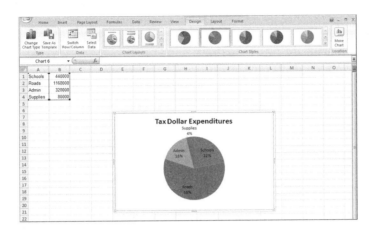

A box appears around the chart. Small dots, called a *handle*, shows at each corner and in the middle of each line. To move your chart and have it fit on one page, do the following.

8. Click and hold the left mouse button inside the **Chart Area**. Make sure it is <u>not</u> the **Plot Area**. A 4-way arrow will show in the chart. As you move the chart it will show as an open box.

9. With your mouse button still depressed, move your chart so the upper left corner is in cell C1.

10. Put your mouse arrow on the handle in the middle of the right line. You should have a horizontal line with an arrow on both ends.

11. Click the mouse, hold down and drag to the middle of column I.

The chart is now next to the data and will fit on one page.

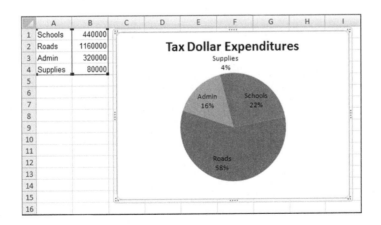

12. To print the spreadsheet and chart without the gridlines, click anywhere off the chart. On the **Page Layout** tab, in the **Sheet Option**s group, make sure the check for **Print Gridline** is not selected. If there is a check mark, click to remove it.

To print the spreadsheet and chart, click anywhere off the chart. From the **File tab** pull down menu, click on **Print**. Rrom the **Print** dialogue box click on the **Print** icon.

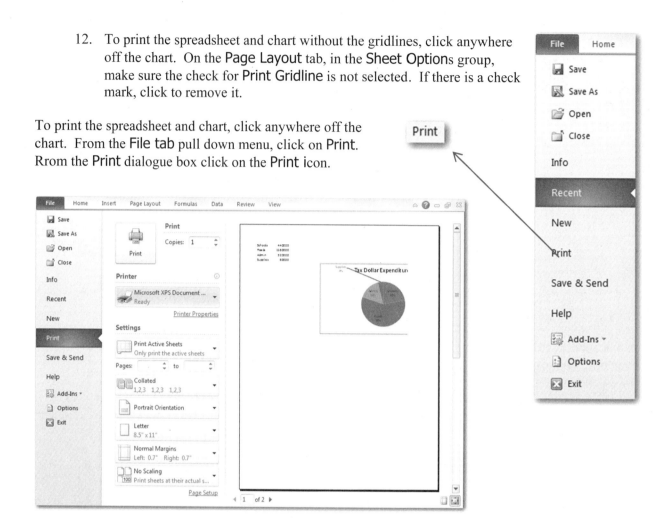

Save your file as **pie-cht**. To do so, do the following:

13. From the **File tab**, select **Save As**. In the **Save in** dialog box make sure your desired location is the active drive.

If your desired location is not active, click on the desired location in the left-hand window.

14. Once your location is active, click on the **File name** text box and key **pie-cht** in the text box. You may need to delete the existing name. Click **Save**.

Example 2. Do the following to change the chart to a horizontal bar chart:

1. Click your mouse anywhere inside the chart. The handles will show on the box. Click the **right** mouse button. A menu will appear.

2. Select Change Chart Type. Select Bar. Select the 1st bar type, Clustered Bar. Click OK.

3. From the Layout tab, in the Labels group, select Data Labels. At the bottom of the pull down list, choose More Data Label Options. Under Label Options, deselect the checkmark next to Category Name. Click Close.

4. From the Layout tab, in the Axis group, choose Gridlines. Choose Primary Vertical Gridlines. From the pulldown list choose None-Do not display Vertical Gridlines.

The data now shows as a horizontal bar chart.

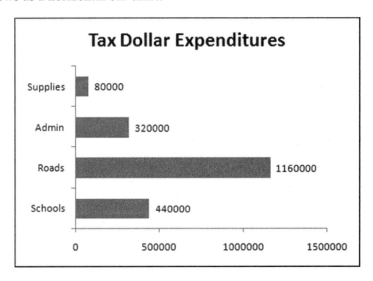

To print just the chart, make sure the handles show on the chart box. From the **File tab** pull down list, click on the **Print** icon. If the handles do *not* show on the chart box, *both* the spreadsheet and chart will print.

To display the expenditures in reverse order, do the following:

5. Make sure the handles show on the chart box.

6. Place your mouse arrow on the Vertical (Category) Axis of the graph. Make sure it is an arrow not a plus sign.

7. Click on your **right** mouse button. Choose Format Axis. Under Axis Options, select the check box for Categories in reverse order. Under Horizontal Axis Crosses: select At maximum category. Click Close.

The expenditures are now reversed.

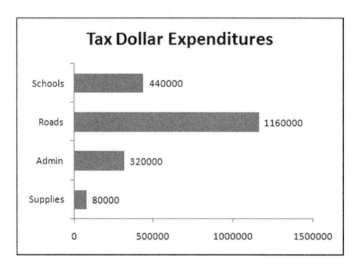

Example 3. Do the following to change the chart to a vertical bar (column) chart:

1. Make sure the handles show on the chart box.

2. Click the **right** mouse button. Select Change Chart Type. Select Column. Choose the 1st chart, Clustered Column. Click OK.

The data now shows in the form of a vertical bar (column) chart.

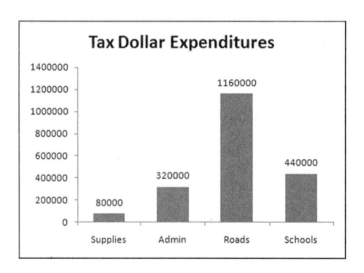

If you wish, save your file as **chart-1**. Close your file.

Simple Histograms

Example 4. The annual imports of a selected group of electronic suppliers are shown in the following frequency distributions.

Imports ($millions)	Number of suppliers
$ 2 up to $5	6
5 up to 8	13
8 up to 11	20
11 up to 14	10
14 up to 17	1

Portray the imports in the form of a histogram.

1. First determine the midpoint of each range in the import column, then use that midpoint for the x-axis data. This is given to you below.

2. On a new worksheet, enter the data as shown below.

	A	B	C	D	E	F	G	H	I
1	Imports	Suppliers							
2	3.5	6							
3	6.5	13							
4	9.5	20							
5	12.5	10							
6	15.5	1							
7									

3. With your mouse arrow on A1, click and drag to highlight **A1:B6**.

4. From the Insert tab, in the Charts group select Column.

5. Select the 1st chart, Clustered Column.

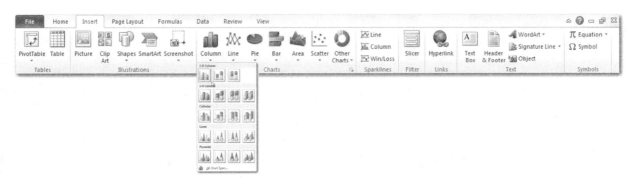

6. Move the chart so the upper left corner is in cell C1 and move the right border to the middle of column I so it will fit on one page. Refer to steps 8–11 on page 15 if needed.

7. From the **Design** tab, in the **Data** group, choose **Select Data**. In the **Select Data Source** dialog box, under **Legend Entries (Series)**, select, **Imports**. Then select the **Remove button**. (We don't want the Imports as part of the values).

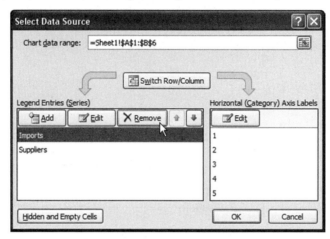

8. In the same **Select Data Source** dialog box, under **Horizontal (Category) Axis Labels**, click **Edit**.

9. An **Axis Labels** dialog box will show. Put your cursor on cell A2, click, hold and drag to cell A6. There will be a running box around cells **A2:A6**. Click **OK**. This identifies the first column as the x-axis labels. Click **OK**.

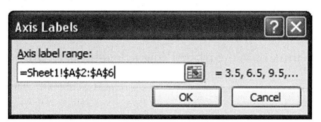

10. From the **Design** tab, **Chart Layouts** group, click on the **down arrow**. Choose **Layout 8**.

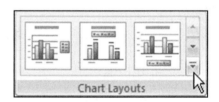

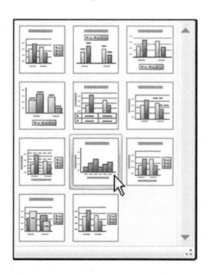

This displays your chart in the form of a histogram.

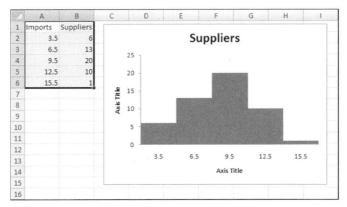

11. In your chart, click on the Chart Title, Suppliers. A box appears around it. Key **Annual Imports of Electronic Suppliers.** As you type the title shows in the equation box. Push <Enter>. The title is displayed in the chart.

12. In the chart, click on the Vertical (Value) Axis Title. Key **Number of Suppliers**. Push <Enter>

13. In the chart, click on the Horizontal (Category) Axis Title. Key **Annual Imports ($millions)**. Push <Enter>

14. From the Layout tab, in the Axes group, choose Gridlines. Choose Primary Horizontal Gridlines. From the pull down list choose Major Gridlines, Display Horizontal Gridlines for Major units.

This completes your chart.

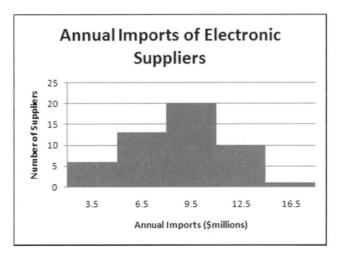

As shown you can use a column chart to create a simple histogram. Excel has a histogram analysis tool to determine a frequency distribution table and prepare a histogram chart from raw data, but that will not be included in this introductory chapter on charts.

If you wish, save your file as **chart-2**. Close your file.

Line Charts

Example 5. The net sales of Klassy Fashions for the years 2000–2009, in thousands of dollars, are:

Year	Net sales (in thous.)
2000	123.4
2001	144.1
2002	201.9
2003	232.4
2004	311.2
2005	410.8
2006	466.9
2007	512.7
2008	552.8
2009	557.6

To visual the data as a line chart, do the following:

1. On a new worksheet, key **Year** in cell A2, **Net Sales** in B1 and **in thous** in B2. Key **2000** and **2001** in cells A3:A4.

2. Highlight **A3:A4.** Place your cursor on the lower right box. The cursor will change to a thick black plus sign. Click, hold and drag the cursor to A12. The rest of the dates are automatically filled in.

3. In cells B3:B12 enter the dollar amounts.

4. Highlight **A3:B12**.

5. From the Insert tab, in the Charts group select Line.

6. Select the 1st upper left chart.

7. Move the chart so the upper left corner is in cell C1 and move the right border to the middle of column I so it will fit on one page. Refer to steps 8–11 on page 15 if needed.

8. From the Design tab, in the Data group choose Select Data. In the Select Data Source dialog box, under Legend Entries (Series), select, Series 1. Then select the Remove button. (We don't want the years as part of the values).

9. In the same Select Data Source dialog box, under Horizontal (Category) Axis Labels, click Edit. An Axis Labels dialog box will show. Put your cursor on cell A3, click, hold and drag to cell A12. There will be a running box around cells **A3:A12**. Click OK. This identifies the first column as the x-axis labels. Click OK.

10. From the Design tab in the Chart Layouts group, click on the down arrow. Choose Layout 10.

11. Place your cursor on Series 2 Legend Entry. Click your right mouse button. Select Delete.

12. In your chart, click on the Chart Title. A box appears around it. Key **Klassy Fashions Net Sales.** As you type the title shows in the equation box. Push **<Enter>**. The title is displayed in the chart.

13. In the chart, click on the Vertical (Value) Axis Title. Key **Net Sales**. Push <Enter>

14. In the chart, click on the Horizontal (Category) Axis Title. Key **Years**. Push <Enter>

15. If the horizontal gridlines do not show do the following: From the Layout tab, in the Axes group, choose Gridlines. Choose Primary Horizontal Gridlines. From the pull down list choose Major Gridlines, Display Horizontal Gridlines for Major units

A line chart is printed that shows the Net Sales trend over the 10 year period.

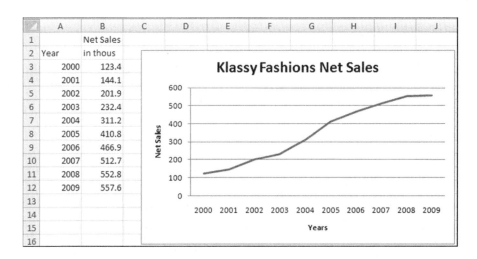

You will now erase just the chart so that you can add more information to the problem.

16. To erase just the chart click your right mouse in the Chart Area.

17. Select Cut.

The chart should now be erased.

Adding additional information

Example 6. Assume the previous net sales figures are for Klassy Fashions Store in Memphis. Assume they opened a new store in Dallas in 2002. Add the new information so you can compare the net sales for the two stores.

1. Click your mouse arrow anywhere in row 3. From the Home tab in the Cells group, click on the down arrow next to Insert. Select Insert Sheet Rows. A new row is inserted above the sales figures.

2. Key **Memphis** in cell B3 and key **Dallas** in cell C3.

3. Starting with cell C6, key in the following values.

123.2
179.8
279.4
506.4
798.3
887.1
916.2
928.4

	A	B	C
1		Net Sales	
2	Year	in thous	
3		Memphis	Dallas
4	2000	123.4	
5	2001	144.1	
6	2002	201.9	123.2
7	2003	232.4	179.8
8	2004	311.2	279.4
9	2005	410.8	506.4
10	2006	466.9	798.3
11	2007	512.7	887.1
12	2008	552.8	916.2
13	2009	557.6	928.4

Do the following to make a comparative line chart:

4. Highlight cells **A3:C13**.

5. From the Insert tab, in the Chart group, select Line.

6. Select the 1st upper left chart.

7. Place your mouse arrow inside the Chart Area. There will be a 4-way arrow. Move the chart so the upper left corner is in cell D1.

8. From the Design tab in the Chart Layouts group, click on the down arrow. Choose Layout 10.

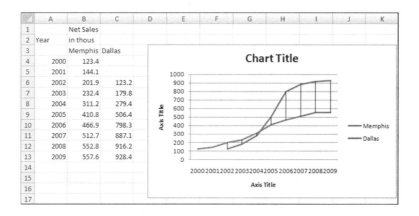

	A	B	C	D	E	F	G	H	I	J	K
1		Net Sales									
2	Year	in thous									
3		Memphis	Dallas								
4	2000	123.4									
5	2001	144.1									
6	2002	201.9	123.2								
7	2003	232.4	179.8								
8	2004	311.2	279.4								
9	2005	410.8	506.4								
10	2006	466.9	798.3								
11	2007	512.7	887.1								
12	2008	552.8	916.2								
13	2009	557.6	928.4								
14											
15											
16											
17											

9. In your chart, click on the Chart Title. A box appears around it. Key **Comparison Chart Memphis and Dallas.** As you type the title shows in the equation box. Push <Enter>. The title is displayed in the chart

10. In the chart, click on the Vertical (Value) Axis Title. Key **Net Sales**. Push <Enter>

11. In the chart, click on the Horizontal (Category) Axis Title. Key **Years**. Push <Enter>

With the comparison line chart you can easily see that the Dallas store sold less than the Memphis store in 2002 when it first opened, but it soon started selling a much greater amount than Memphis.

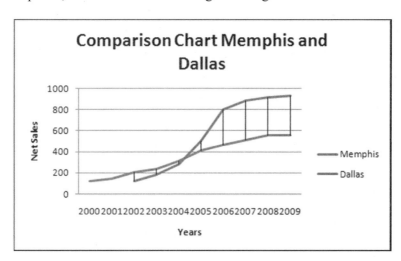

Refining your chart

You can make changes to your chart to give it a different look.

1. Make sure the handles show on the chart.

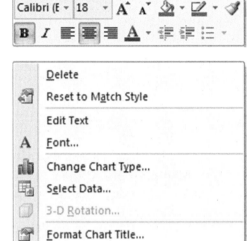

2. Point to the title **Comparison Chart Memphis and Dallas**. Click your **right** mouse. Two dialog boxes appear. Click your mouse on the font size down arrow. Choose **14**.

The title is small and all fits on one line.

3. Point to the **Horizontal (Category) Axis Title**, Years. Right Click your mouse. Select the font size of **12**.

4. Do the same procedure for the **Vertical (Value) Axis Title** of Net Sales. Select the font size of **12**.

5. Click on the **Legend**. It will have handles around it. Click, hold and drag the box down to the bottom right corner of the chart.

6. Click your arrow in the middle of the **Plot Area**. Place your arrow on the middle handle of the right side of the Plot Area and pull it to the right to where the Legend begins.

These steps allow you to make the graph area easier to read.

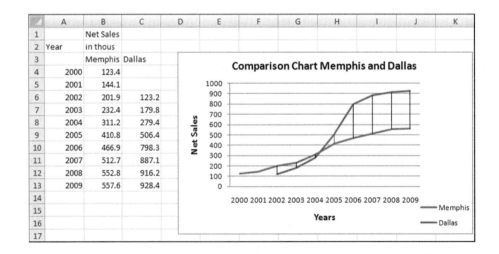

If you want comparison bars instead of comparison lines, do the following:

7. Make sure the handles show on the chart.

8. From the Layout tab, in the Analysis group, click on Up/Down Bars. Choose Up/Down Bars -Show Up Down Bars on a Line Chart.

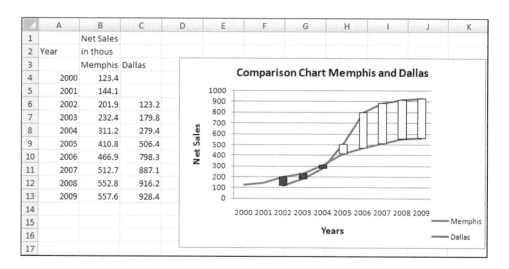

Experiment using the Design, Layout and Format groups. If you make a change and don't like the look, click on the Undo button from the Quick Access Toolbar.

If you wish, save as **chart-3**. Close your file.

As shown below, on the Insert tab, when you click on the Dialogue Launcher arrow at the bottom of the Charts group, there are several chart types that become available.

Dialogue Launcher

Within each of these types or categories of charts, you can choose a variation of the basic charts using the Chart Layout group from the Design tab. They allow you to view your data differently and experiment with your graphic presentations.

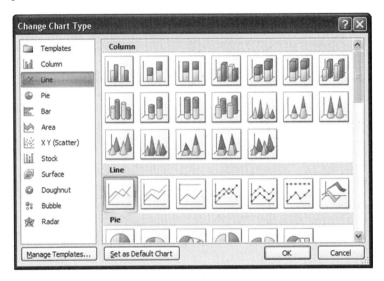

Embedding Charts in a Report

When creating a report describing data, it is often helpful to include a visual illustration. Excel allows you to embed sheets, or charts of information into a Microsoft Word document.

1. Open Microsoft Word for Windows.

2. Prepare your report leaving room for your Excel object. For this report key **The Clayton County Commissioners want to design a chart to show the taxpayers attending the forthcoming meeting what happens to their tax dollars.**

3. From the File tab, select Save As. In the Save in dialog box, make sure your location is selected. In the File name text box, key **budget**. Click Save.

4. Minimize Word by clicking minimize in the top right corner of your screen. It looks like a small line and says Minimize beneath it when your mouse arrows rests on it.

5. Open Microsoft Excel if you are not already in it. Create the report you want to use in your Word document. In this case you will retrieve a file you created earlier.

6. From the File tab, select pie-chart from the Open folder.

7. Highlight **A1:I16**, to highlight the data and/or chart. From the Home tab, in the Clipboard group, select Cut. Minimize Excel by clicking on minimize in the top right hand corner of your screen.

8. Activate Word again by clicking on the Microsoft Word bar at the bottom of the screen.

9. Position your cursor at the point you wish to insert the report. From the Home tab in the Clipboard group, click on the down arrow of the Paste command. Select Paste Special. Select Microsoft Excel Worksheet Object. Click OK.

10. Place your mouse arrow on the chart. You can resize the chart with the handles.

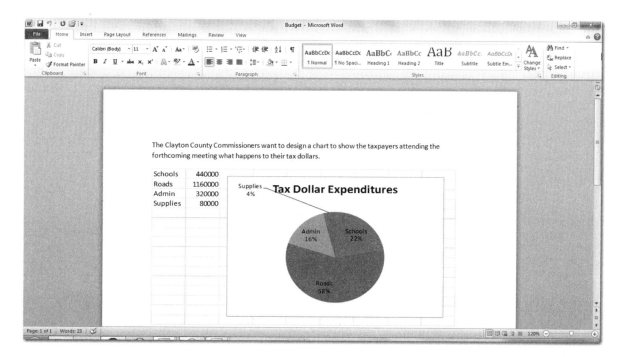

Save your file as **budget**. Close your file. Exit Word. Open Excel. When you close the file pie-cht, respond No, you do not want to save the changes on the clip board.

Practice Exercises taken from textbook. (Put all related data in a single column.)

2-1. A headline in a newspaper reported that crime was on the decline. Listed below are the numbers of homicides from 1993 to 2009. This problem is not in your textbook, but gives you an opportunity to draw a line chart.

Year	Homicides	Year	Homicides
1993	21	2002	35
1994	34	2003	30
1995	26	2004	28
1996	42	2005	25
1997	37	2006	21
1998	37	2007	19
1999	44	2008	23
2000	45	2009	27
2001	40		

Draw a line chart to summarize the data.

2-2. One of the most popular candies in the United States is M&M's, which are produced by the Mars Company. In the beginning M&M's were all brown; more recently they were produced in red, green, blue, orange, brown and yellow. Recently the purchase of a 14 ounce bag of M&M's Plain had 444 candies with the following breakdown by color: 130 brown, 98 yellow, 96 red, 35 orange, 52 blue, and 33 green. Develop a bar chart depicting this information. (Similar to Textbook problem 2-49)

2-3. The following frequency distribution represents the number of frequent flier miles, reported in thousands, for employees of Brumley Statistical Consulting, Inc during the first quarter of 2005. (Textbook problem 2-17)

Frequent Flier Miles (000)	Number of Employees
0 up to 3	5
3 up to 6	12
6 up to 9	23
9 up to 12	8
12 up to 15	2
Total	50

Construct a histogram.

2-4. A recent survey showed that the typical American car owner spends $2,950 per year on operating expenses. Below is a breakdown of the various expenditure items. Draw a pie chart to portray the data. (Textbook problem 2-39) Hint: Abbreviate the Expenditure items to fit in one column.

Expenditure item	Amount
Fuel	$ 603
Interest on car loan	279
Repairs	930
Insurance and license	646
Depreciation	492
Total	$2,950

CHAPTER

3

DESCRIBING DATA: NUMERICAL MEASURES

CHAPTER GOALS

After completing this chapter, you will be able to:

1. Explain the characteristics and uses of measures of location.

2. Use Excel to calculate the arithmetic mean, median, mode, and the weighted mean.

3. Explain the characteristics and uses of measurements of dispersion.

4. Use Excel's Descriptive Statistics Analysis ToolPak to find measures of location and dispersion.

5. Define each measurement found in Excel's Descriptive Statistics Analysis ToolPak Output Table.

Introduction

Over 100 years ago H. G. Wells noted that "statistical thinking will one day be as necessary for efficient citizenship as the ability to read and write." That day has arrived. Today, we cannot avoid being bombarded with all sorts of numerical data. Statistical techniques are used extensively in almost all career fields: social science, physical science, marketing, accounting, quality control, health science, education, professional sports, and politics to name just a few. This chapter will show how easy it is to use Excel to find measures of location (central tendency) and dispersion, measures that are essential to using and understanding statistical data.

Measures of Location: We will use Excel to find a single value or an average to describe a set of data. This single value is referred to as a measure of location. We often need a single number to represent a set of data – one number that can be thought of as being "typical" of all the data. Most people think of arithmetic mean when they hear the word average. However, there are several measures that show the central value of a set of data. The measures of location shown in this chapter that you can use Excel commands to find are the arithmetic mean, the median, the mode, and the geometric mean. We will also create a template to find weighted mean.

The **arithmetic mean** is the most commonly used measure of central tendency. When you total your examination grades and divide by the number of exams, you have computed the arithmetic mean, or average. What follows is an example of how to compute a mean using this formula. For example, during an agonizing quarter, Sam Wise received the following grades on 9 exams in college algebra (arranged in ascending order): 2, 7, 11, 20, 30, 40, 55, 71, and 71. Sam's mean semester grade, then, was $(2 + 7 + 11 + 20 + 30 + 40 + 55 + 71 + 71) \div 9 = 34.111$ or 34, rounded.

The **median** is a measurement of position. If you arrange a series of values in either ascending or descending order, the middle figure in the array of values is called the median. In the case of Sam's grades, the middle or median grade was 30. Both the mean grade of 34 and the median grade of 30 seem to reveal the same thing: Sam was having great difficulty grasping algebra. Even if Sam's instructor had thrown out Sam's lowest grade, the median grade would have been halfway between 30 and 40, that is, 35, not much change. While Sam's mean grade of 34 differed only slightly from his median grade of 30, it is possible in other cases for the difference between the mean and the median to be substantial.

The **mode** is defined as the most frequently occurring value in a series. In the example of Sam's grade, the mode is 71 (a value that might appeal to Sam, but not his teacher). Although not especially useful in our example, the mode is important to, say, the department store buyer of men's suits who wants to order the most popular styles, colors, and sizes.

The **weighted mean** is a special case of the arithmetic mean. It occurs when one value has more importance or more weight than another. For example, a five credit statistics class is more important to your grade point average (GPA) than a one credit bowling course. If Jose earned a 3.2 in his five credits of statistics, 2.8 in four credits of speech, 3.7 in three credits of literature, and 4.0 in a one credit bowling course, what is his GPA?

$$\bar{x}_w = \frac{\Sigma(wx)}{\Sigma x}$$

$$\bar{x}_w = \frac{(5\times3.2)+(4\times2.8)+(3\times3.7)+(1\times4.0)}{5+4+3+1}$$

$$\bar{x}_w = 3.25385 \; or \; 3.3$$

Measures of Dispersion. If two distributions have the same mean, median, and mode, is there no difference between the distributions? Not necessarily. The distributions below are normal, unimodal, symmetrical, bell (or mound) shaped. They have the same measures of central tendency, but they are not identical. Distribution A has more spread, a greater dispersion or variability than distribution B.

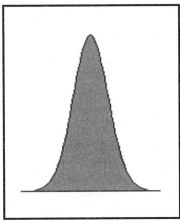

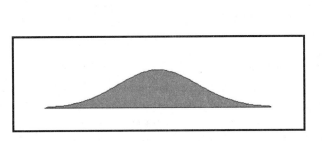

Distribution A

Distribution B

The following is an illustration to help understand the importance of dispersion. An English teacher being pressured to coach a track team does some checking and finds that: the four high-jumpers can only clear an average of 4 feet, the three pole vaulters can only manage an average height of 9 feet, and the average runner can only run the mile in 8 minutes. He concludes that he does not want to manage such a certain failure. Is his assessment accurate? Maybe, but not from the data he collected. Had he looked further, he would have found that one of the four high-jumpers consistently clears 7 feet (good enough for any competition he might face) while the others stumble over 3-foot heights. In the pole vault, one athlete vaults 15 feet, while the others barely explode over a 6-foot bar. And the team has one runner who can break a 4-minute mile. The moral of this tale: without knowledge of dispersion, averages alone do not give a complete picture.

Remember, if one of your feet is frozen in ice (0 degrees Celsius) and the other in almost boiling water (74 degrees Celsius), on average you should be a comfortable 37 degrees Celsius body temperature.

The simplest measure of dispersion is **range**, which is the difference between the highest and lowest values. The most common statistical measurement of dispersion is the **standard deviation** (σ) for population data, and s for sample data, or expressed another way, s is used to approximate σ. The standard deviation is the positive square root of the variance. The variance is the measure of the average squared deviations between each observation and the mean. But what is standard deviation? What does it do, and what does it mean? The above definition really doesn't tell much. Perhaps a better way of defining standard deviation is by looking at how it is applied to the many areas where it is useful.

The empirical rule as illustrated below is a guideline which states, when a distribution of data is normally distributed or approximately mound-shaped, about 68 percent of the data values fall within one standard deviation of the mean, 95 percent fall within two standard deviations, and almost 100 percent (99.7) within three standard deviations

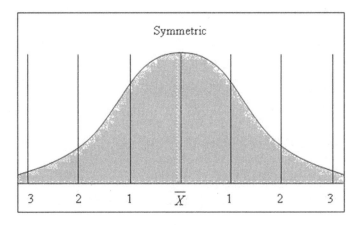

Because many phenomena are distributed approximately in a bell shape, including most human characteristics such as height and weight, the empirical rule is widely used. In the area of quality control, many companies use the mean plus or minus two standard deviations, or the mean plus or minus three standard deviations as cutoff points for acceptance or rejection guidelines.

For example, in 2000 the average fuel consumption rate of automobiles in the United States was 21.2 miles per gallon. If the standard deviation was 5.9 mpg we could use the empirical rule to estimate the distribution of fuel rates of automobiles. About two-thirds (68%) of the fuel consumption rates would fall between 15.3 mpg and 27.1 mpg (21.2 ± 5.9). Ninety-five percent of the fuel rates would fall between 9.4 and 33.0 (21.2 ± two times 5.9). And almost all of the automobiles would have fuel rates between 3.5 and 38.9 mpg (21.2 ± three times 5.9).

Understanding standard deviation is important in statistics.

- It is the most frequently used measure of dispersion. Because of the mathematical properties it possesses, it's more suitable than any other measure of dispersion involving statistical inference procedures.

- It is affected by the value of every observation in a series. A change in the value of any observation will change the standard deviation value. Its value may be distorted by a relatively few extreme values.

- It is often used for making control charts, since most control charts are based on the fact that 95 percent of the normal distribution will fall within plus or minus two standard deviations of the mean. Any item in the distribution that is less than two standard deviations from the mean is considered in control. The difference is attributed to sampling error and chance within the process being used. Any item outside the plus or minus two standard deviations is considered out of control. The difference is attributed to some assignable cause that could be corrected.

Example 1. (mean, median and mode)

Cambridge Power and Light Company selected 20 residential customers. Following are the amounts, to the nearest dollar, the customers were charged for electrical services last month:

54	48	58	50	25	47	75	46	60	70
67	68	39	35	56	66	33	62	65	67

What are the mean, median and mode of these amounts?

1. On a new worksheet, key your data in column A. Key **Example 1** in A1, **Amounts** in A3 and the numbers in A4:A23.

2. In A24:A26, key the labels: **Mean=**, **Median=**, and **Mode=** respectively. Your sheet will look like the example on the right.

In the cell to the right of each label, key the formulas.

3. In B24, key =**AVERAGE(A4:A23)**. Excel uses *average* for the *arithmetic mean*.

4. In B25, key =**MEDIAN(A4:A23)**

5. In B26, key =**MODE(A4:A23)**

Bold the contents of A1. Bold the contents of B24:B26.

	A	B
1	**Example 1**	
2		
3	Amounts	
4	54	
5	48	
6	58	
7	50	
8	25	
9	47	
10	75	
11	46	
12	60	
13	70	
14	67	
15	68	
16	39	
17	35	
18	56	
19	66	
20	33	
21	62	
22	65	
23	67	
24	Mean=	
25	Median=	
26	Mode=	
27		

	A	B	C
1	Example 1		
2			
3	Amounts		
4	54		
5	48		
6	58		
7	50		
8	25		
9	47		
10	75		
11	46		
12	60		
13	70		
14	67		
15	68		
16	39		
17	35		
18	56		
19	66		
20	33		
21	62		
22	65		
23	67		
24	Mean=	54.55	
25	Median=	57	
26	Mode=	67	
27			

The output is as follows:

The average or mean is *54.55*. The median is *57*. (Since there is an even number of data there is no single middle number. The median is the average of the middle *two* numbers, 54 and 60). The mode is *67*.

If there is *no* mode, Excel will display #N/A in that cell. If there is *more than one* mode Excel will display the one that occurs first in the string of data.

On all problems, put your data in a single column. Be sure to include within the parentheses the cell references that contain the data.

Example 2. (weighted mean)

Carter Construction Company pays its hourly employees either $16.50, $19.00, or $25.00 per hour. There are 26 hourly employees, 14 are paid at the $16.50 rate, 10 at the $19.00 rate, and 2 at the $25.00 rate. What is the weighted mean hourly rate paid the 26 employees?

1. In C1, key **Example 2.**

2. Key **Employee** in C3, **Rate** in D3, **Product** in E3, **Weighted** in C8 and **mean=** in C9.

3. Key **14,10**, and **2** in C4:C6 respectively.

4. Key **16.5**, **19**, and **25** in D4:D6 respectively.

5. In E4, key =**C4*D4**.

6. Make E4 your active cell. Place your cursor on the bottom right handle. You will have a thick black plus sign. Click and drag to E5:E6.

7. Highlight **C4:C6**. From the Home tab, in the Editing group choose AutoSum.

8. Highlight **E4:E6**. From the Home tab, in the Editing group choose AutoSum.

9. In D9, key =**E7/C7**.

Bold the contents of C1 and D9. Your output will look as follows.

◢	A	B	C	D	E
1	**Example 1**		**Example 2**		
2					
3	Amounts		Employees	Rate	Product
4	54		14	16.5	231
5	48		10	19	190
6	58		2	25	50
7	50		26		471
8	25		Weighted		
9	47		Mean=	**18.1154**	
10	75				
11	46				
12	60				
13	70				
14	67				
15	68				
16	39				
17	35				
18	56				
19	66				
20	33				
21	62				
22	65				
23	67				
24	Mean=	54.55			
25	Median=	57			
26	Mode=	67			

Formula view allows you to view the formulas and functions within a cell, rather than the output value. To toggle between normal view and formula view, hold down the control key while tapping the tilde key (located above the tab key on most keyboards).

You may have to adjust the column width to be able to view the entire formula. You can also use the Formulas tab. In the Formula Auditing group Choose Show Formulas.

The following is an example of the same page in formula view.

Remember: to switch back to normal view, hold down the control key and tap the tilde key.

	A	B	C	D	E
1	Example 1		Example 2		
2					
3	Amounts		Employees	Rate	Product
4	54		14	16.5	=C4*D4
5	48		10	19	=C5*D5
6	58		2	25	=C6*D6
7	50		=SUM(C4:C6)		=SUM(E4:E6)
8	25		Weighted		
9	47		Mean=	=E7/C7	
10	75				
11	46				
12	60				
13	70				
14	67				
15	68				
16	39				
17	35				
18	56				
19	66				
20	33				
21	62				
22	65				
23	67				
24	Mean=	=AVERAGE(A4:A23)			
25	Median=	=MEDIAN(A4:A23)			
26	Mode=	=MODE(A4:A23)			
27					

Excel's Descriptive Statistics Analysis ToolPak allows you to find the mean, standard error, median, mode, standard deviation, sample variance, kurtosis, skewness, range, minimum, maximum, sum, count, largest number by position, smallest number by position, and the level of confidence simply by entering the numerical data. You probably need to install the Data Analysis tools the first time you use it. If Analysis Tools doesn't appear in the Add-Ins available list box, you may need to Browse. If you get prompted that the Analysis ToolPak is not currently installed on your computer, click Yes to install it.

To demonstrate how to use Excel to compute measures of central tendency and dispersion, here is a typical example:

Dave's Automatic Door Installations installs automatic garage door openers. The following list indicates the number of minutes needed to install a sample of 10 doors: 28, 32, 24, 46, 44, 40, 54, 38, 32, and 42.

1. On a new worksheet, key **Minutes** in A1. Key the rest of your data in column A.

Use instructions 2 – 4 to install the Data Analysis Tools. If they are already available, start with instruction 5.

2. Click the **File tab**. Click **Excel Options** at the bottom of the pull down list.

3. At the <u>left</u> select **Add-Ins.** At the bottom, in the **Manage** box, select **Excel Add-Ins.** Select **Go.** (If Excel Add-Ins does not show, click on the down arrow.)

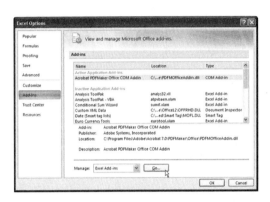

4. From the <u>Add-Ins available</u> list, click on the **Analysis ToolPak** check box, click **OK.**

The Data Analysis Tools should now be available for use.

5. From the **Data** tab, in the **Analysis** group select **Data Analysis.** Select **Descriptive Statistics.** Click **OK.**

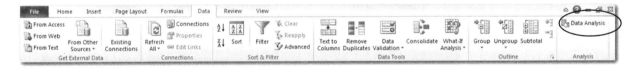

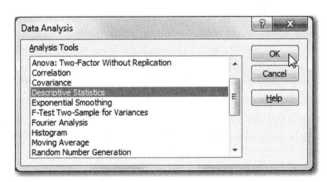

6. For Input Range: key **A1:A11**. Or you may click your mouse on cell A1 then hold and drag to highlight cells A1:A11. Your input range will vary depending on the number in your sample.

7. Grouped by Columns should be selected.

8. Select Labels in first row. If the first row does not contain a label, make sure that the check box is not selected.

9. Select Output Range. Select the text box, key in **C1**.

10. Select Confidence Level for Mean. Select the text box. In this instance, key in **90**.

11. Select Summary statistics.

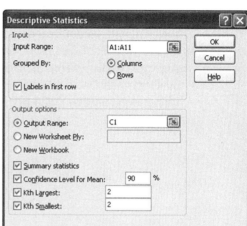

12. Select Kth Largest. Select the text box. In this instance, key in **2**.

13. Select Kth Smallest. Select the text box. In this instance, key in **2**. Click on OK.

(New Worksheet Ply and New Workbook should not be selected.)

The descriptive statistics have been computed automatically.

	A	B	C	D	E
1	Minutes			Minutes	
2	28				
3	32		Mean	38	
4	24		Standard E	2.875181	
5	46		Median	39	
6	44		Mode	32	
7	40		Standard E	9.092121	
8	54		Sample V:	82.66667	
9	38		Kurtosis	-0.43626	
10	32		Skewness	0.133047	
11	42		Range	30	
12			Minimum	24	
13			Maximum	54	
14			Sum	380	
15			Count	10	
16			Largest(2)	46	
17			Smallest(:	28	
18			Confiden	5.270532	
19					

HINT: After you get your results, cross-check the *count* in the output table to make sure it contains the correct number of sample items.

To make your chart easier to read do the following:

1. Place your mouse arrow in the column heading between columns C, and D. The arrow will change to a thick black plus sign. Double click your left mouse button. Column C will automatically widen to accommodate the longest description.

2. Activate cell D4. From the **Home** tab, **in the Number** group place your mouse pointer on the **Decrease Decimal** icon. Click your left mouse button three times. The Standard Deviation is now rounded to three decimals places and is easier to read.

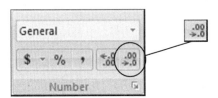

3. Format cells, D7, D8, D9, D10, and D18 to all have three decimal places.

The chart is now easier to read.

	A	B	C	D	E
1	Minutes		Minutes		
2	28				
3	32		Mean	38	
4	24		Standard Error	2.875	
5	46		Median	39	
6	44		Mode	32	
7	40		Standard Deviation	9.092	
8	54		Sample Variance	82.667	
9	38		Kurtosis	-0.436	
10	32		Skewness	0.133	
11	42		Range	30	
12			Minimum	24	
13			Maximum	54	
14			Sum	380	
15			Count	10	
16			Largest(2)	46	
17			Smallest(2)	28	
18			Confidence Level(90.0%)	5.271	
19					

Chapter 3 focuses on measures of location (or central tendency) and dispersion but since the output table displays additional terms that we use in future chapters, we have taken this opportunity to define what Excel displays.

Excel's Descriptive Statistics Output Table contains three measures of location: mean, median and mode. The **Mean** (38) is computed by dividing the sum (380) by the count (10).

The **Median** (39) is a measurement of position in a ranked set of data. It is the middle number in a data set with an odd number of values. In an even set of numbers, it is the value halfway between the two middle values.

The **Mode** (32) is a measurement of frequency, it is the most frequently occurring value. When there are two or more values that appear the same number of times (duplicate modes), Excel reports the value that appears first in the data set. In some data sets, each value is unique so Excel reports "#N/A." The mode is often used with grouped data. A frequency distribution with the highest number of occurrences is called the modal interval.

The output table contains several measures of variation. The **Range** (30) equals the **Maximum** value(54) minus the **Minimum** value(24). Remember, with some data sets the range can be a misleading measure of variation since it only contains the two most extreme values.

The **Standard Deviation** (9.092) is the most common measure of variation or dispersion. In a normal or symmetrical set of data about 68 percent will be within plus or minus one standard deviation of the mean (28.908 – 47.092), 95 percent will be within plus or minus two standard deviations of the mean (19.816 – 56.184), and almost all of the data (99.7 percent) will be within plus or minus three standard deviations of the mean (10.724 – 65.276).

The **Variance** is the standard deviation squared. Excel's output table shows the sample standard deviation and variance computed using *n-1* in the denominator. To find the *population* standard deviation and the *population* variance, computed by using *n* as the denominator, use the STDEVP and VARP functions.

The **Largest (2)** and the **Smallest (2)** values in Excel's output table are the second longest (46) and the second shortest (28) installation times. These values can be used to eliminate outliers. They can also be use to estimate quartiles in data with a large number of frequencies. For example if you had 1600 in your data set you would divide the count (1600) by 4 and enter 400 as the largest and the smallest. The output table would then show the approximate third and first quartile .

The **Standard Error** (2.875) shown on the output table will be used more extensively later in our exercises. The standard error is the standard deviation divided by the square root of the sample size. It is a measure of uncertainty about the mean, and is used for statistical inference (confidence intervals, regression belts, and hypothesis tests.)

The **Confidence Level (90.0%)** (5.271) is half of the 90% confidence interval for the mean. In this measurement we can be 90% confident that the interval, 32.729 minutes to 43.271 minutes, will contain the population parameter or the true mean installation time.

Kurtosis (–0.436) measures the degree of peakedness in symmetric distributions. If a symmetric distribution is more peaked than the normal distribution, that is, if there are fewer values in the tails, the kurtosis measure is negative. If the distribution is flatter than the normal distribution, that is if there are more values in the tails than a corresponding normal distribution, the kurtosis measure is positive. (For more details on how Excel computes kurtosis search Help for "KURT function").

Skewness (0.133) is a measurement of the lack of symmetry in a distribution. If there are a few extreme small values and the tail of the distribution runs off to the left we say the distribution is negatively skewed and our skewness value would be negative. If there are a few extremely large values and the tail of the distribution runs off to the right, we say the distribution is positively skewed and the skewness value would be positive. The formula for finding skewness used by Excel is different than the Pearson's Coefficient of Skewness used in the Statistical Techniques in Business and Economics textbook. (Excel computes the skewness value using the third power of the deviations from the mean. For more details on how Excel computes skewness search Help for "SKEW function").

Practice Exercises taken from textbook. (Put all related data in a single column.)

3-1. The accounting firm of Crawford and Associates has five senior partners. Yesterday the senior partners saw six, four, three, seven, and five clients respectively. Compute the mean number and median number of clients seen by a partner. (Textbook Problem 3-49)

3-2. Owens Orchards sells apples in a large bag by weight. A sample of seven bags contained the following number of apples: 23, 19, 26, 17, 21, 24, 22. Compute the mean number and median number of apples in a bag. (Textbook Problem 3-50)

3-3. Trudy Green works for the True-Green Lawn Company. Her job is to solicit lawn-care business via the telephone. Listed below is the number of appointments she made in each of the last 25 hours of calling. (Textbook Problem 3-54)

9	5	2	6	5	6	4	4	7	2	3	6	3
4	4	7	8	4	4	5	5	4	8	3	3	

What is the arithmetic mean number of appointments she made per hour? What is the median number of appointments per hour?

3-4. The American Diabetes Association recommends a blood glucose reading of less than 130 for those with Type 2 diabetes. Blood glucose measures the amount of sugar in the blood and Type 2 diabetes often appears in older adults. Below are the readings for February for a recently diagnosed senior citizen. (Textbook Problem 3-58)

112	122	116	103	112	96	115	98	106	111
106	124	116	127	116	108	112	112	121	115
124	116	107	118	123	109	109	106		

  a. What is the arithmetic mean glucose reading?
  b. What is the median glucose reading?
  c. What is the modal glucose reading?

3-5. The Loris Healthcare System employs 200 persons on the nursing staff. Fifty are nurse's aids, 50 are practical nurses, and 100 are registered nurses. Nurse's aids receive $8 an hour, practical nurses $15 an hour, and registered nurses $24 an hour. What is the weighted mean hourly wage?
(Textbook Problem 3-15)

3-6. The Split-A-Rail Fence Company sells three types of fences to homeowners in suburban Seattle, Washington. Grade A costs $5.00 per running foot to install, Grade B costs $6.50 per running foot, and Grade C, the premium quality, costs $8.00 per running foot. Yesterday, Split-A-Rail installed 270 feet of Grade A, 300 feet of Grade B, and 100 feet of Grade C. What was the weighted mean cost per foot of fence installed? (Textbook Problem 3-55)

3-7. A sample of households that subscribe to the United Bell Phone Company revealed the following numbers of calls received last week: (Textbook Problem 3-51)

52	43	30	38	30	42	12	46
39	37	34	46	32	18	41	5

Using a confidence level of 95%, and a largest and smallest K of 4, use Excel to find the measures of central tendency and dispersion.

3-8. The Citizens Banking Company is studying the number of times the ATM located in a Lebalaw's Supermarket at the foot of Market Street is used per day. Following are the number of times the machine was used over each of the last 30 days: (Textbook Problem 3-52)

83	64	84	76	84	54	75	59	70	61
63	80	84	73	68	52	65	90	52	77
95	36	78	61	59	84	95	47	87	60

Using a confidence level of 90%, and a largest and smallest K of 10, use Excel to find the measures of central tendency and dispersion.

CHAPTER

4

DESCRIBING DATA: DISPLAYING AND EXPLORING DATA

CHAPTER GOALS

After completing this chapter, you will be able to:

1. Develop and interpret quartiles, deciles and percentiles.

2. Compute and understand the coefficient of skewness.

3. Define the measurements found in Excel's Descriptive Statistics Analysis ToolPak Output Table.

4. Use Excel to draw and interpret a scatter diagram.

Introduction

Chapter 3 introduced you to several measures of location such as the mean and the median that allow us to report a typical value in a set of observations. You also computed several measures of dispersion such as mean and standard deviation that allow us to describe the variation or spread in a set of data. We continue with descriptive statistics in this chapter.

Although the standard deviation is the most used measure of dispersion it is sometimes useful to divide a set of observations into equal parts and measure positions using **quartiles**, **deciles** or **percentiles**. The first, second and third quartiles divide a set of observations into four equal parts. Remember in Chapter 3 when we arranged a set of data from smallest to largest the middle point was the median. When we arrange a set of data from smallest to largest and divide it into 4 equal parts the value below which 25 percent of the observations occur is the first quartile. The middle point, the median, is the second quartile. The value below which 75 percent of the observations occur is the third quartile. The middle 50 percent of the data, the **quartile range**, is between the first quartile and the third quartile.

Deciles and percentiles are also measurements of position. After arranging the data into an ordered array from smallest to largest if we divide it into 10 equal parts we have deciles and if we divide it into 100 equal parts we have percentiles. If your income was in the 7th decile you could conclude that 70 percent of the people have a lower income and 30 percent have a higher income. If your friend finished in the 42nd percentile in the Boston Marathon then she finished ahead of 42 percent of the runners and behind 58 percent of the runners.

Another characteristic of a set of data is its shape. The shape is **symmetrical** if the mean and the median are the same and the data is spread evenly so that the data values below and above the mean and median are mirror images of each other such as the illustrations of dispersion in Chapter 3. The shape is positively skewed when the mean is larger than the median and the values extend further to the right of the peak. The shape is negatively skewed when the mean is smaller than the median and the data extends further to the left of the peak. When a set of data has two peaks it is bimodal, three peaks tri-modal and etc.

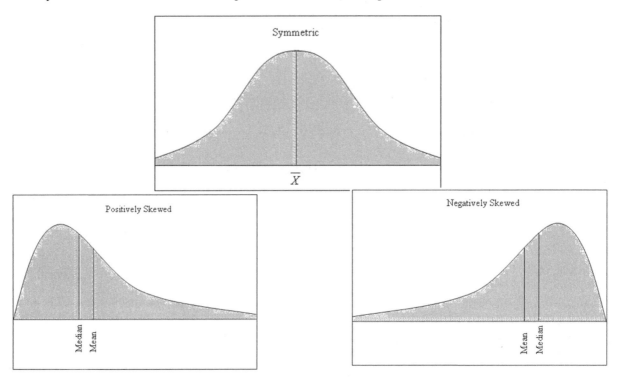

To demonstrate how to use Excel to compute measures of central tendency, dispersion, position and shape here is a typical example.

Example 1. The quality control department of a jelly and jam company is responsible for checking the weight of the 8-ounce jars of raspberry Jam. The weights of a sample of 13 jars are:

7.68   7.82   8.12   8.03   7.89   7.93   8.09   7.75   7.88   8.01   8.11   7.99   8.03

1. On a new worksheet, key **Weight** in cell A1. Key the rest of your data in column A.

2. From the **Data** tab, in the Analysis group select **Data Analysis**. Select **Descriptive Statistics**. Click **OK**.

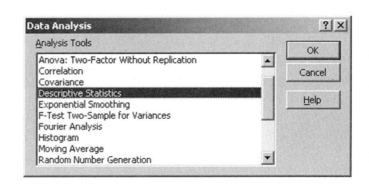

If Data Analysis does not show, use instructions 2-4 on Page 43 to install the Add-Ins, then select Data Analysis and Descriptive Statistics.

3. For Input Range:, key **A1:A14**. Or you may click your mouse on cell A1 then hold and drag to highlight cells A1:A14. Your input range will vary depending on the number in your sample.

4. Grouped by Columns, should be selected.

5. Select Labels in first row. If the first row does not contain a label, make sure that the check box is not selected.

6. Select Output Range. Select the text box, key in **C1**.

7. Select Summary statistics.

8. Select Confidence Level for Mean. Select the text box, in this instance key in **90**.

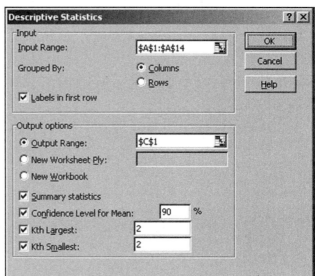

9. Select Kth Largest. Select the text box, in this instance key in **2**.

10. Select Kth Smallest. Select the text box, in this instance key in **2**. Click OK.

(New Worksheet Ply and New Workbook should not be selected.)

The descriptive statistics have been computed automatically.

HINT: After you get your results, cross-check the *count* in the output table to make sure it contains the correct number of sample items.

To make your chart easier to read do the following:

1. Place your mouse arrow in the column heading between columns C, and D. The arrow will change to a thick black plus sign. Double click your left mouse button. Column C will automatically widen to accommodate the longest description.

2. Place your mouse arrow in the column heading D. The arrow will be a thick down arrow. Click your left mouse button. The entire D column will be highlighted.

3. From the Home bar, in the Cells group select Format. At the bottom, select Format Cells. The Number tab should be selected.

4. Under Category:, select Number. In the Decimal places: text box, key in **3**. Or click on the up arrow to 3. Click on OK.

The chart is now easier to read.

	A	B	C	D	E
1	Weight		*Weight*		
2	7.68				
3	7.82		Mean	7.948	
4	8.12		Standard Error	0.038	
5	8.03		Median	7.990	
6	7.89		Mode	8.030	
7	7.93		Standard Deviation	0.139	
8	8.09		Sample Variance	0.019	
9	7.75		Kurtosis	-0.532	
10	7.88		Skewness	-0.603	
11	8.01		Range	0.440	
12	8.11		Minimum	7.680	
13	7.99		Maximum	8.120	
14	8.03		Sum	103.330	
15			Count	13.000	
16			Largest(2)	8.110	
17			Smallest(2)	7.750	
18			Confidence Level(90.0%)	0.069	
19					

Chapter 4 focuses on location and shape but since the output table displays additional terms, we have taken this opportunity to define what Excel displays, like we did in Chapter 3.

Excel's Descriptive Statistics Output Table contains three measures of central tendency: mean, median and mode. The **Mean** (7.948) is computed by dividing the sum (103.330) by the count (13).

The **Median** (7.990) is a measurement of position in a ranked set of data. It is the middle number in a data set with an odd number of values. In an even set of numbers, it is the value halfway between the two middle values.

The **Mode** (8.030) is a measurement of frequency, it is the most frequently occurring value. When there are two or more values that appear the same number of times (duplicate modes), Excel reports the value that appears first in the data set. In some data sets, each value is unique so Excel reports "#N/A." The mode is often used with grouped data. A frequency distribution with the highest number of occurrences is called the modal interval.

The output table contains several measures of variation. The **Range** (.440) equals the **Maximum** value (8.120) minus the **Minimum** value(7.680). Remember, with some data sets the range can be a misleading measure of variation since it only contains the two most extreme values.

The **Standard Deviation** (.139) is the most common measure of variation or dispersion. In a normal or symmetrical set of data about 68 percent will be within plus or minus one standard deviation of the mean (7.809 – 8.087), 95 percent will be within plus or minus two standard deviations of the mean (7.670 – 8.226), and almost all of the data (99.7 percent) will be within plus or minus three standard deviations of the mean (7.531 – 8.365).

The **Variance** is the standard deviation squared. Excel's output table shows the sample standard deviation and variance computed using *n-1* in the denominator. To find the *population* standard deviation and the *population* variance, computed by using *n* as the denominator, use the STDEVP and VARP functions.

The **Largest (2)** and the **Smallest (2)** values in Excel's output table are the second largest (8.110) and the second smallest (7.750) weight. These values can be used to eliminate outliers. They can also be use to estimate quartiles in data with a large number of frequencies. For example if you had 1600 in your data set you would divide the count (1600) by 4 and enter 400 as the largest and the smallest. The output table would then show the approximate third and first quartile. If the data is arranged in order from smallest to largest and you divide count (1600) by ten you would have the 160th item as the first decile and 1440th item as the ninth decile. You could also divide by 100 and estimate percentiles.

The **Standard Error** (0.038) shown on the output table will be used more extensively later in our exercises. The standard error is the standard deviation divided by the square root of the sample size. It is a measure of uncertainty about the mean, and is used for statistical inference (confidence intervals, regression belts, and hypothesis tests.)

The **Confidence Level (90.0%)** (.069) is half of the 90% confidence interval for the mean. In this measurement we can be 90% confident that the interval, 7.879 ounces to 8.017 ounces, will contain the population parameter or the true mean weight.

Kurtosis (–0.532) measures the degree of peakedness in symmetric distributions. If a symmetric distribution is more peaked than the normal distribution, that is, if there are fewer values in the tails, the kurtosis measure is negative. If the distribution is flatter than the normal distribution, that is if there are more values in the tails than a corresponding normal distribution, the kurtosis measure is positive. (For more details on how Excel computes kurtosis search Help for "KURT function").

Skewness (–0.603) is a measurement of the lack of symmetry in a distribution. If there are a few extreme small values and the tail of the distribution runs off to the left we say the distribution is negatively skewed and our skewness value would be negative. If there are a few extremely large values and the tail of the distribution runs off to the right, we say the distribution is positively skewed and the skewness value would be positive. The formula for finding skewness used by Excel is different than the Pearson's Coefficient of Skewness used in the Statistical Techniques in Business and Economics textbook. (Excel computes the skewness value using the third power of the deviations from the mean. For more details on how Excel computes skewness search Help for "SKEW function").

Scatter Diagrams

When we study a single variable we refer to it as **univariate** data. When we want to look at two variables and see if they may have a relationship we refer to this as **bivariate** data. Examples of bivariate questions would be: Is there a relationship between money spent on advertising and sales? What is the relationship between age and income? Do tall parents have tall children? A **scatter diagram** is often used to visualize the relationship between two variables. To draw a scatter diagram we scale one variable along the horizontal axis (X-axis) of a graph and the other variable along the vertical axis (Y-axis). Chapter 13 will go into more details on scatter diagrams and on measuring the relationship between bivariate data. There are a couple of cautions when using scatter diagrams. First, the data must be at least interval scale. Second, be aware that the scale you use for the vertical and horizontal axis, can affect the apparent visual strength of the relationship.

Example 2. An appliance store has outlets in several large metropolitan areas. The general sales manager plans to air a commercial for a digital camera on selected local TV stations prior to a sale starting on Saturday and ending Sunday. She plans to get the information for Saturday-Sunday digital camera sales at the various outlets and pair them with the number of times the advertisement was shown on the local TV stations. The purpose is to find whether there is a relationship between the number of times the advertisement was aired and digital camera sales. The pairings are:

Location of TV Stations	Number of Airings	Saturday-Sunday Sales ($ thousands)
Buffalo	4	15
Albany	2	8
Erie	5	21
Syracuse	6	24
Rochester	3	17

1. On a new worksheet, enter the data for the problem as shown below. Notice that the data for # of Airings is entered first since it is the independent variable.

2. Highlight **B2:C6**.

3. From the Insert tab, in the Charts group select Scatter.

4. Select the 1st upper left chart, Scatter with only Markers.

5. From the Design tab in the Chart Layouts choose Layout 1.

6. Move the chart so the upper left corner is in cell D1 and move the right border to the middle of column I so it will fit on one page.

7. Place your cursor on Series 1 Legend Entry. Click your right mouse button. Select Delete.

8. In your chart, click on the Chart Title. A box appears around it. Key **Correlation Between Number of TV Ads and Sales.** As you type, the title shows in the equation box. Push <Enter>. The title is displayed in the chart.

9. In the chart, click on the Vertical (Value) Axis Title. Key **Sales (in thousands)**. Push <Enter>

10. In the chart, click on the Horizontal (Category) Axis Title. Key **Number of Airings**. Push <Enter>

11. Point to the title Correlation Between Number of TV Ads and Sales. Click your **right** mouse. Two dialog boxes appear. Click your mouse on the font size down arrow. Choose 14.

The completed chart is now displayed.

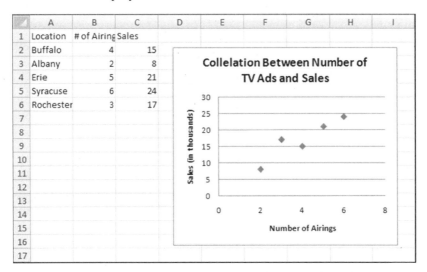

As you can see from the scatter diagram there is appositive relationship between the number of times the advertisement was aired and digital camera sales. In chapter 13 we will study the relationship between the variables.

Chapter 4

Practice Exercises taken from textbook. (Put all related data in a single column.)

4-1. The Thomas Supply Company, Inc is a distributor of gas powered generators. As with any business, the length of time customers take to pay their invoices is important. Listed below, arranged from smallest to largest, is the time in days for a sample of The Thomas Supply Company, Inc. invoices   (Textbook Problem 4-5)

    13 13 13 20 26 27 31 34 34 34 34 35 35 36 37 38
    41 41 41 45 47 47 47 50 51 53 54 54 56 62 67 82

Use Excel's Descriptive Statistics Output Table to find the mean, standard error, median, mode, standard deviation, sample variance, kurtosis, skewness, range, minimum, maximum, sum count, largest (2), smallest (2), and estimate quartile one, quartile two, the first decile, and the ninth decile and the 67th percentile.

4-2. Kevin Horn is the national sales manager for National Textbooks, Inc. He has a sales staff of 40 who visit college professors all over the United States. Each Saturday morning he requires his sales staff to send him a report. This report includes, among other things, the number of professors visited during the previous week. Listed below, ordered from smallest to largest, are the number of visits last week. (Textbook Problem 4-6)

    38 40 41 45 48 48 50 50 51 51 52 52 53 54 55 55 55 56 56 57
    59 59 59 62 62 62 63 64 65 66 66 67 67 69 69 71 77 78 79 79

Use Excel's Descriptive Statistics Output Table to find the mean, standard error, median, mode, standard deviation, sample variance, kurtosis, skewness, range, minimum, maximum, sum count, largest (2), smallest (2), and estimate quartile one, quartile two, the first decile, and the ninth decile and the 33rd percentile

4-3. Using Excel, develop a scatter diagram for the following sample data. How would you describe the relationship between the values? (Textbook Problem 4-15)

X-Value	Y-Value
10	6
8	2
9	6
11	5
13	7
11	6
10	5
7	2
7	3
11	7

4-4. An auto insurance company reported the following information regarding the age of a driver and the number of accidents reported last year. Using Excel, develop a scatter diagram for the data below and write a brief summary. (Textbook Problem 4-31)

Age	Accidents
16	4
24	2
18	5
17	4
23	0
27	1
32	1
22	3

CHAPTER
5
A SURVEY OF PROBABILITY CONCEPTS

CHAPTER GOALS

After completing this chapter, you will be able to:

1. Define and use the counting techniques to find permutations.

2. Define and use the counting techniques to find combinations.

3. Use Excel to find the number of permutations in a subset.

4. Use Excel to find the number of combinations in a subset.

Introduction

Chapter 5 of the textbook explains the principles of probability – a number between zero and one that describes the relative possibility (chance or likelihood) an event will occur. It explains the two different approaches to probability, **subjective**, and **objective**. Subjective probability is based on intuition, feelings, or judgment. Objective probability is subdivided into (1) **classical probability** and **empirical probability**. Classical or a priori is based on the assumption that the outcomes of an experiment are equally likely. That is, they are built into the experiment such as tossing a coin. When you toss a fair coin, the probability of a head is ½ or .5 and the probability of a tail is ½ or .5. Empirical, which is sometimes called relative frequency, posterior, or historical probability is based on records and past experience.

If events are **mutually exclusive** they can not occur simultaneously. With one flip of a coin you get a head or a tail. **Collectively exhaustive** means that the sample space must contain all possible outcomes. If events are **independent**, one result does not influence the other result. When I flip a coin, the second flip is independent of the results of my first flip. Using the coin-flipping concept, we could say that the **compliment** of getting a head is getting a tail.

The words "**and**" and "**independent**" are used with the **multiplication rules** of probability. The **general rule of multiplication** states that the probability of events "A" and "B" which are not independent is the probability of event "A" times the probability of event "B/A." For example using a deck of fifty-two cards, the probability of being dealt four aces in a row without reshuffling would be 4/52 times 3/51 times 2/50 times 1/49. The **special rule of multiplication** states that events which are independent is the probability of event "A" times the probability of event "B." For example, the probability of being dealt four aces in a row with reshuffling would be 4/52 times 4/52 times 4/52 times 4/52.

The words "**or**" and "**mutually exclusive**" are used with the **addition rules of probability**. The **general rule of addition** states that the probability of events "A" or "B" when the events are not mutually exclusive is the probability of "A" plus the probability of "B" minus the probability of "A" and "B." For example, the probability of a king or spade in a deck of fifty-two cards would be: The probability of a king (4/52) plus the probability of a spade (13/52), minus the probability of the king of spades (1/52). The **special rule of addition** states that the probability of events "A" or "B" when the events are mutually exclusive is the probability of "A" plus the probability of "B." For example, the probability of a king or a queen is 4/52 plus 4/52.

Conditional probability is the probability of an event taking place given information that is revised. The textbook uses a tree diagram and the formula for Bayes' Theorem to explain conditional probability.

Spreadsheets using Excel would be advantageous to accomplish the arithmetic needed to solve the above problems if they were repetitive. However, when doing one or two problems a calculator is more convenient.

The formulas for the **counting techniques** of finding **combinations** and **permutations** are built into Excel. Excel, therefore, is useful to find how many subsets can be obtained from a set. In selecting the elements in the subsets, the distinction between combinations and permutations depends on whether the order of the selection makes a difference. The numbers 1, 2, and 3 are different permutations when arranged as 123 or 321 because order is important. However, 123 and 321 are the combinations of 1, 2, and 3 when order is not important. If we divide a class of 27 students into groups or teams of three, each team of three students would be a combination, because the team would be the same people regardless of the order. If we wanted to know how many ways we could park 5 cars in 21 empty parking spaces. The answer would be a permutation since order is important. If Sam's car is next to the front door that is different than if Joan's car is next to the front door.

Permutations and Combinations

When you use Excel to find permutations and combinations, the dialog box fills most of the screen. The cell that is active when you access the different functions is the cell in which the results will be displayed. Be sure to identify your work.

Example 1. The Betts Machine Shop, Inc., has eight screw machines but only three spaces available in the production area for the machines. In how many different ways can the eight machines be arranged in the three spaces available?

On a new worksheet, key the following as shown on the following page.

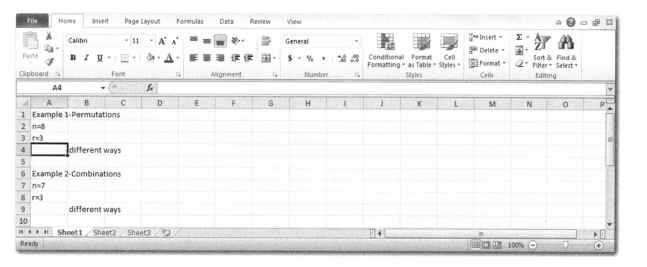

Make A4 your active cell.

1. Click on the Insert Function icon that is located at the top and to the left of the formula bar.

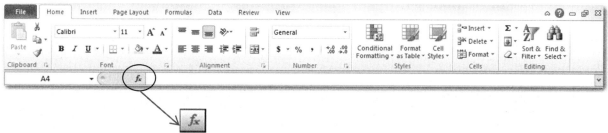

The Insert Function dialog box is displayed.

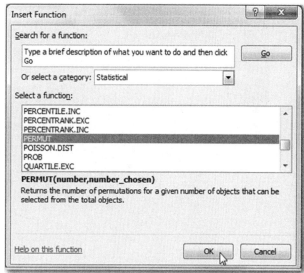

2. Click your mouse arrow on the down arrow of the Or select a category: scroll bar. Select Statistical.

3. Click your mouse arrow on the down arrow of the Select a function: scroll bar. Select PERMUT.

4. Click OK.

The second dialog box contains several text boxes to fill.

The *Number* text box is the number of objects, commonly referred to as *n*.

The *Number_chosen* text box is the number of objects in each permutation, commonly referred to as *r*.

5. Your cursor should be on the **Number** text box. Key **8**. Touch the **tab** key.

6. In the **Number_chosen** text box, key **3**.

As soon as you enter the number in the Number_chosen text box, the permutation shows after *Formula result =* in the lower left corner of the dialog box.

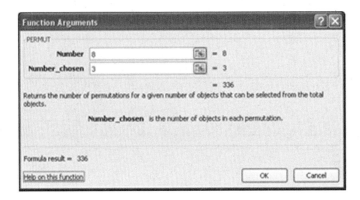

7. Click **OK**.

The permutation of 336 is displayed in cell A4.

Bold the contents of A1 and A4.

	A	B	C	D	E	F	G	H	I
1	**Example 1-Permutations**								
2	n=8								
3	r=3								
4	**336**	different ways							
5									
6	Example 2 - Combinations								
7	n=7								
8	r=3								
9		different combinations							
10									

Example 2: The marketing department has been given the assignment of designing color codes for the different lines of CDs sold by Goody Records. The three colors are to be used on each CD, but a combination of three colors used for one cannot be rearranged and used to identify a different CD. This means that if green, yellow, and violet were used to identify one line, then yellow, green, and violet (or any combination of these three colors) cannot be used to identify another line. How many different combinations could be created from seven colors?

On the same worksheet make A9 your active cell.

1. Click on the Insert Function icon to the left of the formula bar.

2. Click your mouse arrow on the down arrow of the Or select a category scroll bar., select Math & Trig.

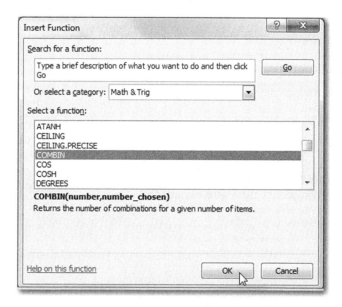

3. Click your mouse arrow on the down arrow of the Select a function: scroll bar, select COMBIN.

4. Click OK.

The second dialog box contains several text boxes to fill.

The *number* text box is the number of items commonly referred to as *n*.

The *number_chosen* text box is the number of objects in each combination, commonly referred to as *r*.

5. Your cursor should be on the number text box. Key **7**. Touch the **tab** key.

6. In the number_chosen text box, key **3**.

As soon as your last data is entered, the combination shows after *Formula result* = in the lower left corner of the dialog box.

> 7. Click **OK**.

The combination value of 35 is displayed in cell A9.

Bold the contents of A6 and A9.

	A	B	C	D	E	F	G	H	I
1	**Example 1-Permutations**								
2	n=8								
3	r=3								
4	336	different ways							
5									
6	**Example 2 - Combinations**								
7	n=7								
8	r=3								
9	35	different combinations							
10									

If you wish, save your file as **permcomb**.

You can put several different problems on one worksheet. Just be sure the cell in which you want the result is the active cell when you access the Paste Function.

Practice Exercises taken from textbook.

5-1. For the daily lottery game in Illinois, participants select three numbers between 0 and 9. A number cannot be selected more than once, so a winning ticket could be, say, 307, but not 337. Purchasing one ticket allows you to select one set of numbers. The winning numbers are announced on TV each night. How many different outcomes (three-digit numbers) are possible? (Textbook Problem 5-66)

5-2. A national pollster has developed 15 questions designed to rate the performance of the President of the United States. The pollster will select 10 of these questions. How many different arrangements are there for the order of the 10 questions? (Textbook Problem 5-39)

5-3. A representative of the Environmental Protection Agency (EPA) wants to select samples from 10 landfills. She has 15 landfills from which she can collect samples. How many different samples are possible? (Textbook Problem 5-38)

5-4. A company is creating three new divisions and seven managers are eligible to be appointed head of a division. How many different ways could the three new heads be appointed? Hint: Assume the division assignment makes a difference. (Textbook Problem 5-40)

CHAPTER

6

DISCRETE PROBABILITY DISTRIBUTIONS

CHAPTER GOALS

After completing this chapter, you will be able to:

1. Define and use discrete probability distributions.

2. Use Excel to create discrete probability distributions.

3. Use Excel to find binomial probabilities.

4. Use Excel to find Poisson distributions.

Introduction

Chapter 2 showed you how you can use Excel to graphically portray data in pie charts, bar charts, histograms, line charts, etc. Chapter 3 emphasized descriptive statistics with measurements of central tendency and dispersion. That chapter was concerned with descriptive statistics, describing something that had already occurred.

Chapter 5 introduced us to probability concepts. Chapter 6 turns to the second facet of statistics, that is, computing the chance or probability that something *will* occur. This facet of statistics is referred to as **inferential statistics** or **statistical inference.**

Statistical inference makes a statement about a population based on a sample taken from that population. Any time we use statistical inferences there is a chance of making an error or being wrong. *Probability theory* scientifically evaluates the risks involved in making these inferences. Probability theory allows the decision maker with only limited information to analyze the risks and minimize the gamble inherent in such things as marketing a new product or accepting a shipment containing defects.

This chapter will show how you can use Excel to find three different **discrete distributions**: the **binomial distribution,** the **hypergeometric distribution** and the **Poisson distribution** to model and analyze real-world processes. These distributions involve discrete random variables, variables that can assume only certain clearly separated values resulting from counts of an item of interest. The number of rooms in a house, the number of people in a room, and the number of pop cans purchased for a party are all discrete random variables. These are different from **continuous distributions** which deal with continuous random variables that can assume any value in an interval. Such measurements as width of a room, the height of a person, and the amount of pop in a can of Coke are all examples of continuous random variables. In the next chapter we will discuss continuous distributions.

Here are a few examples of discrete probability distributions and how they are used.

Binomial Distribution

1. An outcome on each trial of an experiment is classified into one of two mutually exclusive categories – a success or a failure.
2. The random variable counts the number of successes in a fixed number of trials.
3. The probability of success and failure stay the same for each trial.
4. The trials are independent, meaning that the outcome of one trial does not affect the outcome of any other trial.

When you use Excel to find various statistical functions, the dialog box fills most of the screen. The cell that is active when you access the different functions is the cell in which the result will be displayed. On a new worksheet, key the following as shown:

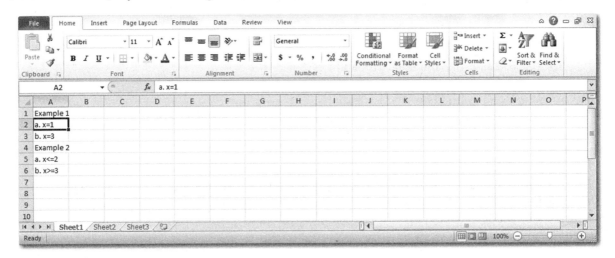

Make B2 your active cell.

To use the binomial distribution function of Excel, do the following:

1. Click on the **Insert Function** icon to the left of the formula bar.

The Insert Function dialog box is displayed.

2. Click your mouse arrow on the down arrow of the Or select a category: scroll bar. Select Statistical.

3. From the Select a function: list box, select BINOM.DIST. Click on OK.

The BINOM.DIST dialog box contains several text boxes to fill.

The *Number_s* text box is for the number of observed successes, commonly referred to as x.

The *Trials* text box is for the number of trials, commonly referred to as n.

The *Probability_s* text box is for the probability of success on each trial, commonly referred to as π.

The *Cumulative* text box is used to indicate whether x, the number of observed successes, is cumulative or not cumulative. You would key 1 for true if you want the cumulative probability that includes the numbers up to and including the value of x. You would key 0 for false (or not cumulative) if x is the number of observed successes only.

You will use the step 2 dialog box to solve the following problem:

Example 1. In a binomial distribution, n = 5 and π = .20, determine the following probabilities: (a) $x = 1$, (b) $x = 3$.

1. Your cursor should be on the Numbers_s text box. Key **1**. Touch the tab key.

2. In the Trials text box, key **5**. Touch the tab key.

3. In the Probability_s text box, key **.20** . Touch the tab key.

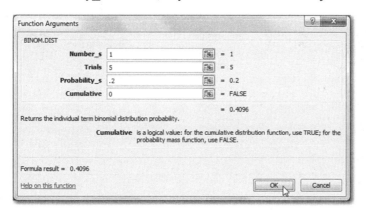

4. In the Cumulative text box, since you want exactly 1 observed success, key **0** for false (not cumulative).

As soon as you enter the number in the Cumulative text box, the probability shows after the Formula result = in the lower left corner of the dialog box.

5. Click OK.

The probability value of .4096 is displayed in cell B2.

To complete part b of example 1, make B3 your active cell. Repeat the previous steps but key **3** for the value of *x* in the Number_s text box. You should get a probability value of .0512.

Make cell B5 your active cell.

You will use the BINOM.DIST function to solve the following problem.

Example 2. In a binomial distribution, where n = 8 and π = .30, determine the following probabilities:
(a) $x \leq 2$, (b) $x \geq 3$.

1. Follow the steps from the previous exercise.

2. Your cursor should be in the number_s text box. Key **2**. Touch the tab key.

3. In the trials text box, key **8**. Touch the tab key.

4. In the probability_s text box, key **.30**. Touch the tab key.

5. Your cursor should be in the cumulative text box, since you want to select cumulative (0 through 2 inclusive), key **1** for true.

6. Click OK.

The probability value of .551774 is now displayed in cell B5.

Make cell B6 your active cell. Key in the formula = **1-B5**. Touch the <Enter> key. The value .448226, which is the compliment of $x \leq 2$, is displayed. This is the answer to part (b) of Example 2.

	A	B	C	D	E	F	G	H	I	
1	Example1									
2	a. x=1	0.4096								
3	b. x=3	0.0512								
4	Example2									
5	a. x<=2	0.551774								
6	b. x>=3	0.448226								
7										

If you wanted to know the probability for *x* being < 2, you would use *x* = 1 in the Number_s text box and 1 (or true) for the Cumulative text box. This would give you the probabilities for 0 and 1 inclusive, which is less than 2.   You can use the BINOM.DIST function and the complement of the probability (subtracted from 1) to solve binomial distributions.

Print your first two examples if you wish.

Example 3. Assume a binomial distribution where n = 5 and π = .30. List the probabilities of a success for values of *x* from 0 to 5.

1. Starting with cell D1, key in the information for Example 3 as shown below.

	A	B	C	D	E	F	G	H	I
1	Example1			Example3					
2	a. x=1	0.4096			probability				
3	b. x=3	0.0512		x	of occurrence				
4	Example2			0					
5	a. x<=2	0.551774		1					
6	b. x>=3	0.448226		2					
7				3					
8				4					
9				5					
10									

2. Make cell E4 your active cell.

3. Select the BINOM.DIST function as shown earlier. Your cursor should be on the Numbers_s text box. Key **D4**. Touch the tab key.

4. In the Trials text box, key **5**. Touch the tab key.

5. In the Probability_s text box, key **.30**. Touch the tab key.

6. In the Cumulative text box, key **0**. Click on OK.

The probability of .16807 shows in cell E4. Place your mouse arrow on the lower right handle of cell E4. It will change to a thick black plus sign. Click, hold and drag the cursor to cell E9. The probability amounts have been automatically filled in. From the Home tab, in the Editing group, click on the AutoSum icon. Note that the probabilities are collectively exhaustive. That is, they add up to 1 or 100%.

	A	B	C	D	E	F	G	H	I
1	Example1			Example3					
2	a. x=1	0.4096			probability				
3	b. x=3	0.0512		x	of occurrence				
4	Example2			0	0.16807				
5	a. x<=2	0.551774		1	0.36015				
6	b. x>=3	0.448226		2	0.3087				
7				3	0.1323				
8				4	0.02835				
9				5	0.00243				
10					1				
11									

As Example 3 shows, you can use Excel to create tables. Make sure you have a cell reference in the Number_s text box instead of a value.

Chapter 6

Poisson Distribution

1. The random variable is the number of times some event occurs during a defined interval.
2. The probability of the event is proportional to the size of the interval.
3. The intervals do not overlap and are independent.

Example 4. In a Poisson distribution $\mu = 4$, (a) what is the probability that x = 2? (b) what is the probability that x $\leq$ 2? (c) what is the probability that x > 2?

In cell A11 key **Example 4**. In Cell A12 key **a. x=2** In cell A13 key **b. x<=2**. In cell A14 key **c. x>2**. Make cell B12 your active cell.

To use the Poisson distribution function of Excel, do the following:

1. Click on the **Insert Function** icon to the left of the formula bar.

2. From the **Or select a category:** list box, select **Statistical**.

3. Click your mouse arrow on the down arrow of the **Select a function:** scroll bar. Select **POISSON.DIST**.

4. Click **OK**.

Step 2 of the POISSON.DIST dialog box contains several text boxes to fill.

The *X* text box is for the number of occurrences (successes).

The *Mean* text box is for the arithmetic mean number of occurrences (successes) in a particular interval of time, commonly referred to as (mu) μ.

The ***Cumulative*** text box is used to indicate whether *X*, the number of occurrences (successes) is cumulative or not cumulative. You would key 1 for true (cumulative) or 0 for false (not cumulative).

You will use the step 2 dialog box to continue this example.

5. Your cursor should be in the *X* text box. Key **2**. Touch the **tab** key.

6. In the **Mean** text box, key **4**. Touch the **tab** key.

7. In the **Cumulative** text box, key **0**.

8. Click **OK**.

The probability of .146525 is now displayed in cell B12.

Make B13 your active cell. Repeat steps 1 – 8 but key **1** in the cumulative text box. You should get a probability of .238103. Make cell B14 your active cell. Key **=1-B13**. Touch the <Enter> key. The value .761897 is displayed, which is the compliment of x <=2. This is the answer to part (c) of Example 4.

◢	A	B	C	D	E	F
1	Example 1			Example 3		
2	a. x=1	0.4096		x	probability	
3	b. x=3	0.0512			of occurance	
4	Example 2			0	0.16807	
5	a. x<=2	0.551774		1	0.36015	
6	b. x>=3	0.448226		2	0.3087	
7				3	0.1323	
8				4	0.02835	
9				5	0.00243	
10					1	
11	Example 4					
12	a. x=2	0.146525				
13	b. x<=2	0.238103				
14	c. x>2	0.761897				

Print Examples 1 through 4 if you wish. Close your worksheet.

Use discrete distributions to solve the following problems. Be sure to identify your outcome on the worksheet. Also remember that the cell that is active when you work the exercises is the cell in which the results will be displayed.

Practice Exercises taken from textbook.

6-1. An American Society of Investors survey found 30 percent of individual investors have used a discount broker. In a random sample of nine individuals, what is the probability: (Textbook Problem 6-13)

a. Exactly two of the sampled individuals have used a discount broker.
b. Exactly four of them used a discount broker.
c. None of them used a discount broker.

6-2. An auditor for Health Maintenance Services of Georgia reports 40 percent of policyholders 55 years or older submit a claim during the year. Fifteen policyholders are randomly selected from company records. (Textbook Problem 6-39)

a. What is the probability that exactly 10 of the selected policyholders submitted a claim last year?
b. What is the probability more than 10 of the selected policyholders submitted a claim last year?

6-3. In a binomial distribution $n = 12$ and $\pi = .60$. Find the probabilities. (Textbook Problem 6-20)

a. $x = 5$.
b. $x \leq 5$.
c. $x \geq 6$.

6-4. A manufacturer of window frames knows from long experience that 5 percent of the production will have some type of minor defect that will require an adjustment. What is the probability that in a sample of 20 window frames: (Textbook Problem 6-22)

a. None will need adjustment?
b. At least 1 will need adjustment?
c. More than 2 will need adjustment?

6-5. Automobiles arrive at the Elkhart exit of the Indiana Toll Road at the rate of two per minute. The distribution of arrivals approximates a Poisson distribution. (Textbook Problem 6-28)

a. What is the probability that no automobiles arrive in a particular minute?
b. What is the probability that at least one automobile arrives during a particular minute?

6-6. In the past, schools in Los Angeles County have closed an average of three days each year for weather emergencies. What is the probability that schools in Los Angeles County will close for four days next year? (Textbook Problem 6-30)

6-7. Recent crime reports indicate that 3.1 motor vehicle thefts occur each minute in the United States. Assume that the distribution of thefts per minute can be approximated by the Poisson probability distribution: (Textbook Problem 6-49)

a. Calculate the probability exactly four thefts occur in a minute.
b. What is the probability there are no thefts in a minute?
c. What is the probability there is at least one theft in a minute?

CHAPTER
7
CONTINUOUS PROBABILITY DISTRIBUTIONS

CHAPTER GOALS

After completing this chapter, you will be able to:

1. Define and use normal probability distributions.

2. Use Excel to create a normal probability distribution.

3. Use Excel and the standard normal distribution to determine the probability that an observation will be above or below a value.

4. Use Excel and the standard normal distribution to determine the probability that an observation will lie between two points.

5. Use Excel and the standard normal distribution to find the value of an observation when the percent above or below the observation is given.

Introduction

Chapter 6 dealt with discrete probability distributions. This chapter will continue the study of probability distributions by examining a very important continuous probability distribution, the **normal probability distribution.** As noted in the preceding chapter, a continuous random variable is one that can assume an infinite number of possible values within a specified range. It usually results from measuring something, such as the amount of gasoline in a tank. The number of gallons might be 11.0 gallons, 11.1 gallons, 11.12 gallons, and so on, depending on the accuracy of the measurement. Other continuous variables include weights, time, temperature, length, width, etc. Many measurements tend to follow a "normal" pattern. The weights of the beef patties to make McDonald's Quarter Pounder, the average heights of American men, and the amount of Pepsi in a can are all examples of continuous random variables that tend to be normally distributed. A normal probability distribution is bell-shaped, symmetrical and asymptotic.

Areas Under the Normal Curve

PLEASE NOTE!!

When you use your text to compute the area under a curve, the given area is to the left or right of the *mean*. When using Excel to compute the normal cumulative distribution, the area is cumulative from the *left side* of the curve. Therefore if you want to compute an area between *x* and the mean, you will compute the difference between the given area and .5 (half the area under the curve). In this exercise we will create several worksheet templates that can be used for a variety of purposes.

Example 1. Creating a worksheet (template) to use for finding normal probability distributions.

    1.   On a new worksheet enter the cell contents as shown below.

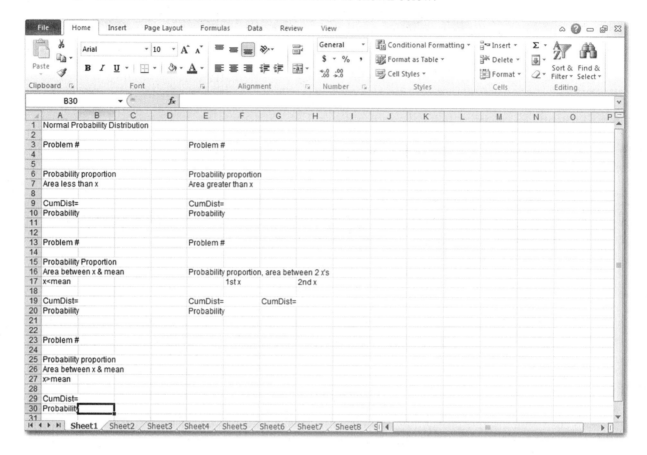

Cells A3:B10 will be used for finding the area less than *x*. Since Excel computes this area automatically, no other computations are needed.

    2.   In cell B20, key **=.5-B19**

Cells A13:B20 will be used when the area is between *x* and the mean, and *x* is less than the mean. Since Excel computes only the area less than *x*, that value must be subtracted from .5 (half the area under the curve) to find the area in between.

    3.   In cell B30, key **=B29-.5**

Cells A23:B30 will be used when the area is between *x* and the mean, and *x* is greater than the mean. Since Excel computes only the area less than *x*, .5 (half the area under the curve) must be subtracted from that value.

    4.   In cell F10, key **=1-F9**

Cells E3:F10 will be used when the area is more than x. Since Excel computes only the area less than x, that value must be subtracted from 1 (the total area under the curve.)

    5.   In cell F20, key **=H19-F19**

Cells E13:H20 will be used when the area is between two values of x. The smaller value of x is used as the 1st number and the larger value of x as the 2nd number, then the two areas are subtracted.

When you are finished with the formulas, the cell contents of your worksheet should look as shown below. Remember, to switch to formula view, hold the control key down while tapping the tilde key. You may have to adjust the column width to be able to view the entire formula. You can also use the Formulas tab. In the Formula Auditing group Choose Show Formulas.

	A	B	C	D	E	F	G	H
1	Normal Probability Distribution							
2								
3	Problem #				Problem#			
4								
5								
6	Probability proportion				Probability proportion			
7	Area less than x				Area greater than x			
8								
9	CumDist=				CumDist=			
10	Probability				Probability =1-F9			
11								
12								
13	Problem #							
14								
15	Probability Proportion							
16	Area between x & mean				Probability proportion, area between 2 x's			
17	x<mean					1st x		2nd x
18								
19	CumDist=				CumDist=		CumDist=	
20	Probability =0.5-B19				Probability =H19-F19			
21								
22								
23	Problem #							
24								
25	Probability proportion							
26	Area between x & mean							
27	x>mean							
28								
29	CumDist=							
30	Probability =B29-0.5							

Save your worksheet as **normprbd**. (If needed, refer to Chapter 1 on how to save.)

When you use Excel's Normal Distribution function, the cell that is active is the cell in which the results will be displayed. Before you choose the function always make sure your active cell is the cell to the right of the cell containing the label CumDist=.

Example 2. The employees of a manufacturing company are awarded efficiency ratings. The distribution of the ratings approximates a normal probability distribution. The mean is 400, the standard deviation 50. (a) What is the area under the normal curve between 400 and 482? (b) What is the area under the normal curve for ratings greater than 482? (c) What is the area under the normal curve for ratings greater than 500?

    1.   If it is not already open, retrieve file **normprbd**.

Since part a is for an area between x and the mean, and x is greater than the mean, you will use cells A23:B30.

    2.   In cell B23, key **Example 2-a**.

    3.   Make B29 your active cell since that is where you want the results to be displayed. Click on the Insert Function icon to the left of the formula bar.

    4.   From the Or select a category: dialog box, select Statistical. Click your mouse arrow on the down arrow of the Select a function: scroll bar. Select NORM.DIST. Click OK.

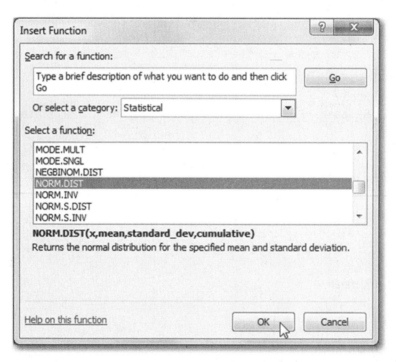

The dialog box for NORM.DIST is displayed.

    5.   The cursor should be on the X text box. Key **482**. Touch the tab key.

    6.   In the Mean text box, key **400**. Touch the tab key.

    7.   In the Standard_dev text box, key **50**. Touch the tab key.

    8.   In the Cumulative text box, key **1** for true. (The cumulative text box will always contain 1) Click OK.

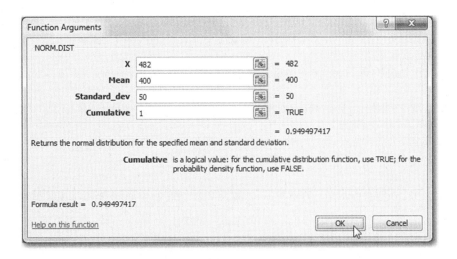

The cumulative distribution is displayed in B29 and the probability (area) is displayed in B30. The area between 400 and 482 is .449497.

9.   Bold the contents of B23.

10.   Bold the contents of B30.

This makes the answer easier to associate with the problem.

If you were to key 0 in the cumulative text box, the resulting value would be the height of the normal density function. If you were to plot the bell curve, this height would be useful for finding the value at which the curve peaks.

Since part b of Example 2 is for an area greater than x you will use cells E3:F10.

11.   In cell F3, key **Example 2-b**.

12.   Make F9 your active cell since you want the results to be displayed in this cell. Click on the Insert Function icon.

13.   From the Or select a category: dialog box, select Statistical. Click your mouse arrow on the down arrow of the Select a function: scroll bar. Select NORM.DIST. Click OK.

You will enter the same data as before.

14.   The cursor should be on the X text box. Key **482**. Touch the tab key.

15.   In the Mean text box, key **400**. Touch the tab key.

16.   In the Standard_dev text box, key **50**. Touch the tab key.

17.   In the Cumulative text box, key **1**. Click OK.

The cumulative distribution is displayed in F9, and the probability (area) is displayed in F10. The area greater than 482 is .050503.

18.   Bold the contents of cells F3 and F10.

Since part c of Example 2 also is for an area greater than x, you will use cells E6:F10 again. Since you don't need the cell contents for the area less than x, you will replace those cells.

19. Highlight **A6:B10**. Touch the <Delete> key.

20. Highlight **E6:F10**. From the Home tab, in the Clipboard group, select the Copy button.

21. Make A6 your active cell. From the Home tab, in the Clipboard group, select the Paste button. Touch the <Enter> key.

The data for Example 2-b is repeated. You will replace the cells with data from Example 2-c.

22. In B3, key **Example 2-c**.

23. Make B9 your active cell. Click on the Insert Function icon.

The completed dialog box from Example 2-b is displayed. Since everything is the same except the data for the x text box, you will change just that data.

24. Click your mouse arrow on the x text box. Use the <Back Space> key to remove the data of 482. Key **500**. Click OK.

25. Bold the contents of B3.

To do another problem that uses the same template, copy and paste the range of cells needed to a different area of your spreadsheet and replace the cell contents as needed.

	A	B	C	D	E	F	G	H
1	Normal Probability Distribution							
2								
3	Problem #	Example 2-c			Problem#	Example 2-b		
4								
5								
6	Probability proportion				Probability proportion			
7	Area greater than x				Area greater than x			
8								
9	CumDist=	0.97725			CumDist=	0.949497		
10	Probability	0.02275			Probability	0.050503		
11								
12								
13	Problem #							
14								
15	Probability Proportion							
16	Area between x & mean				Probability proportion, area between 2 x's			
17	x<mean					1st x		2nd x
18								
19	CumDist=				CumDist=		CumDist=	
20	Probability	0.5			Probability	0		
21								
22								
23	Problem #	Example 2-a						
24								
25	Probability proportion							
26	Area between x & mean							
27	x>mean							
28								
29	CumDist=	0.949497						
30	Probability	0.449497						
31								

Finding the Value of the Observation X when the Percent Above or Below the Observation is Given.

Excel also has a function to find the value of *x* when you know the probability, mean, and standard deviation.

Example 3. The Layton Tire and Rubber Company wishes to set a minimum mileage guarantee on its new MX100 tire. Tests reveal the mean mileage is 67,900 with a standard deviation of 2,050 miles and that the distribution of miles follows the normal probability distribution. They want to set the minimum guaranteed mileage so that no more than 4 percent of the tires will have to be replaced. What minimum mileage should Layton announce?

You will use .04 as the probability. Again, the cell that is active is the cell in which the results will be displayed.

1. On the same worksheet, in E23, key **Example 3**.

2. Make E24 your active cell. Click on the Insert Function icon.

3. From the Or select a category: dialog box, select Statistical. Click your mouse arrow on the down arrow of the Select a function: scroll bar. Select NORM.INV. Click OK.

The dialog box for NORM.INV is similar to the one for NORM.DIST.

4. The cursor should be on the Probability text box. Key **.04**. Touch the tab key.

5. In the Mean text box, key **67900**. Touch the tab key.

6. In the Standard_dev text box, key **2050**. Click OK.

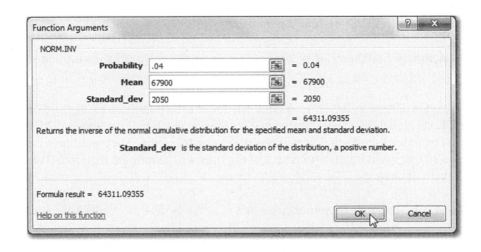

The result of **64311.09** is displayed. Therefore Layton can advertise that it will replace for free any tire that wears out before it reaches 64,312 miles (rounded up to the next mile).

	E24	▼	*fx*	=NORMINV(0.04,67900,2050)			
	A	B	C	D	E	F	G	H
1	Normal Probability Distribution							
2								
3	Problem #	Example 2-c			Problem#	Example 2-b		
4								
5								
6	Probability proportion				Probability proportion			
7	Area greater than x				Area greater than x			
8								
9	CumDist=	0.97725			CumDist=	0.949497		
10	Probability	**0.02275**			Probability	**0.050503**		
11								
12								
13	Problem #							
14								
15	Probability Proportion							
16	Area between x & mean				Probability proportion, area between 2 x's			
17	x<mean					1st x		2nd x
18								
19	CumDist=				CumDist=		CumDist=	
20	Probability	0.5			Probability	0		
21								
22								
23	Problem #	Example 2-a			Example 3			
24					64311.09			
25	Probability proportion							
26	Area between x & mean							
27	x>mean							
28								
29	CumDist=	0.949497						
30	Probability	**0.449497**						
31								

7. Bold the contents of cells E23 & E24.

You can do several problems on one worksheet by deleting and copying cell contents. Just be sure to label your problems. It is also very helpful to bold the cell contents of the exercise number and the corresponding answer.

If you wish, save your file as **nrmex2&3**. Close your file.

Practice Exercises taken from textbook.

7-1. A normal population has a mean of 20.0 and a standard deviation of 4.0. (Textbook Problem 7-13)

a.   What proportion of the population is between 20.0 and 25.0?
b.   What proportion of the population is less than 18.0?

7-2. The number of viewers of *American Idol* has a mean of 29 million with a standard deviation of 5 million. Assume this distribution follows a normal distribution. What is the probability that next week's show will: (Textbook Problem 7-20)

a.   Have between 30 and 34 million viewers?
b.   Have at least 23 million viewers?
c.   Exceed 40 million viewers?

7-3. The accounting department at Weston Materials Inc., a national manufacturer of unattached garages, reports that it takes two construction workers a mean of 32 hours and a standard deviation of 2 hours to erect the Red Barn model. Assume the assembly times follow the normal distribution.
(Textbook Problem 7-36)

a.   What percent of the garages take between 32 hours and 34 hours to erect?
b.   What percent of the garages take between 29 hours and 34 hours to erect?
c.   What percent of the garages take 28.7 hours or less to erect?
d.   Of the garages, 5 percent take how many hours or more to erect?

7-4. The annual commissions earned by sales representatives of the Machine Products Inc., a manufacturer of light machinery, follow the normal probability distribution. The mean yearly amount earned is $40,000 and the standard deviation is $5000. (Textbook Problem 7-40)

a.   What percent of the sales representatives earn more than $42,000 per year?
b.   What percent of the sales representatives earn between $32,000 and $42,000?
c.   What percent of the sales representatives earn between $32,000 and $35,000?
d.   The sales manages wants to award the sales representatives who earn the largest commissions a bonus of $1,000. He can award a bonus to 20 percent of the representatives. To the nearest hundred dollars, what is the cutoff point between those who earn a bonus and those who do not?

7-5. Fast Service Truck Lines uses the Ford Super Duty F-750 exclusively. Management made a study of maintenance costs and determined the number of miles traveled during the year followed the normal distribution. The mean of the distribution was 60,000 miles and the standard deviation was 2,000 miles. (Textbook Problem 7-44)

a. What percent of the Ford Super Duty F-750s logged 65,200 miles or more?
b. What percent of the trucks log more than 57,060 miles but less than 58,280 miles?
c. What percent of the Fords traveled 62,000 miles or less during the year?

7-6. In establishing warranties on HDTV sets the manufacturer wants to set the limits so that few will need repair at manufacturer expense. On the other hand, the warranty period must be long enough to make the purchase attractive to the buyer. For a new HDTV the mean number of months until repairs are needed is 36.84 with a standard deviation of 3.34 months. Where should the warranty limits be set so that only 10 percent of the HDTVs need repairs at the manufacturer's expense? (Textbook Problem 7-52)

CHAPTER

8

SAMPLING METHODS AND THE CENTRAL LIMIT THEOREM

CHAPTER GOALS

After completing this chapter, you will be able to:

1. Use Excel to show that means of small samples have more dispersion or scatter than the means of large samples.

2. Define and construct a sampling distribution of sample means.

3. Use Excel to illustrate the central limit theorem.

Introduction

The law of large numbers tells us that a large sample tends to give a better approximation of the population parameter than a small sample. This reflects a simple notion supported by common sense: In only a few trials, results can be very different, but in a large sample, results tend to be fairly stable and consistent. For example it would not be unusual to get 3 heads when flipping a fair coin 3 times, but it would be very unusual to get 300 heads when flipping a fair coin 300 times. This notion is widely used by insurance companies to estimate the expected amount of claims they will pay in any one year. It is used by government to estimate tax collections. It tells gambling casinos that when the odds favor the house, even a little bit, if they can induce enough people to gamble long enough, the house will win.

The central limit theorem states that when sampling from a normal, a uniform, or even a skewed distribution, the means of the samples will be approximately normally distributed if a sufficient number of samples are taken. The following examples will show you how you can use Excel to work with sampling and sampling distributions.

Sampling From a Normal Population

Example 1. Birth weight of a newborn is a major concern for all new parents. Nationally, the 50th percentile birth weight of children born at full term (40 weeks) is 7.04 pounds. That is, the average or "normal" birth weight of a full term baby is 7.04 pounds. From a random sample of 237 full term babies born at Community Hospital, their mean weight was 7.04 with a standard deviation of .42. To illustrate the law of large numbers from this sample of birth weights, you will:

a. Generate a random frequency distribution of weights.

b. From the frequency distribution, select two small samples and two large samples, and compare the means and standard deviations.

c. Construct histograms using a very small sampling distribution of sample means and a larger sampling distribution of sample means.

a. Generating a Random Distribution

1. On a new worksheet key the data as shown below.

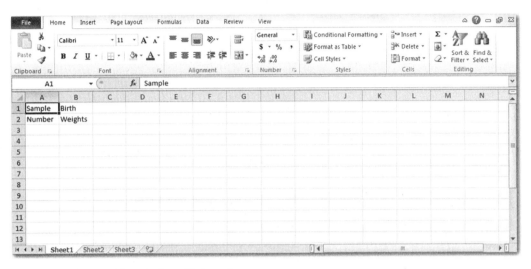

2. In A3, key **1**. Touch the <Enter> key.

3. Make A3 your active cell. From the Home tab, in the Editing group, place your cursor on the Fill icon. It shows as a down arrow. Select Series. From the Series dialog box, select Series in Columns. Select Type Linear. In the Step Value text box, key **1**. In the Stop Value text box, key **237**. Click OK.

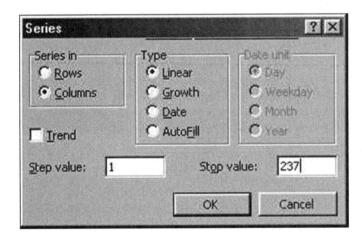

This enters the number 1-237 in A3:A239.

4. In B3, key **=NORM.INV(RAND(),7.04,.42)**. Press <Enter>.

This generates a random number with a mean of 7.04 and a standard deviation of .42.

5. Make B3 your active cell. Place your mouse arrow on the lower right handle of B3. Make sure you have a thick, black plus sign. Click your left mouse button twice, rapidly.

This automatically fills the cells in B4:B239 with random numbers. Touch the F9 (re-calculate) function key on your keyboard. Notice how the random birth weights change each time. Each time you perform a new procedure, the random values change. You need to save the generated numbers so you can select random numbers from them. Your worksheet will look different from the examples that follow.

6. Highlight **A1:B239**. As you drag your mouse pointer below the worksheet it will highlight the lower rows. From the Home tab, in the Clipboard group, select the Copy icon.

7. From File Button, in the middle of the list, select Close. Select Do<u>n</u>'t save for Do you want to save changes. Select Yes for Save a large amount of information to the Clipboard.

8. From the File Button select New, select Blank worksheet, select Create. Make A1 your active cell. From the Home tab, in the Clipboard group, select the Paste icon. Your random numbers should now stay as a population from which to take samples.

b. Sample Sizes and Comparisons

1. In E1:H2, enter the contents as shown below.

	A	B	C	D	E	F	G	H	I
1	Sample	Birth			Sample	Sample	Sample	Sample	
2	Number	Weights			of 3	of 3	of 30	of 30	
3	1	7.403472							
4	2	7.337615							
5	3	6.692735							
6	4	6.8831							
7	5	6.934702							
8	6	7.167506							
9	7	6.587278							
10	8	6.959932							
11	9	6.79725							
12	10	6.684729							

Make sure you have a Data Analysis command in your Data tab. If Data Analysis does not appear, select <u>A</u>dd-Ins. See Page 43, instructions 2 – 4.

2. From the Data tab, in the Analysis group select Data Analysis. Place your mouse arrow on the down arrow of the side scroll bar. Select Sampling. Click OK.

The Sampling dialog box appears.

3. Your cursor should be in the text box for <u>I</u>nput Range. Key **B3:B239**

4. Select <u>R</u>andom. In the Number of Samples text box, key **3**. Select the button for <u>O</u>utput Range. In the <u>O</u>utput Range text box, key **E3**. Click OK.

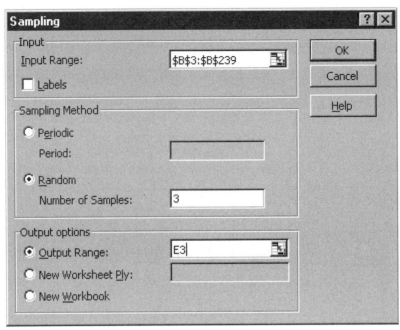

From the random weights in B3:B239, 3 were selected.

5. From the Data tab, in the Analysis group select Data Analysis. Select Sampling. Click OK.

6. Leave the Input Range as **B3:B239**. Leave the Number of Samples as **3**. In the text box for Output Range, replace the contents with **F3**. Click OK.

From the random weights in B3:B239, 3 more were selected.

7. In D6:D7, key **Mean** and **StdDev**, respectively.

8. In E6, key =**Average(E3:E5)**

9. In E7, key =**STDEV(E3:E5)**

10. Highlight **E6:E7**. Drag the lower right handle of E7 to F7.

	A	B	C	D	E	F	G	H	I
1	Sample	Weights			Sample	Sample	Sample	Sample	
2	Number	Weights			of 3	of 3	of 30	of 30	
3	1	7.403472			6.845856	7.04544			
4	2	7.337615			6.758911	6.922607			
5	3	6.692735			6.728874	7.45883			
6	4	6.8831		Mean	6.77788	7.142292			
7	5	6.934702		StdDev	0.060754	0.280925			
8	6	7.167506							
9	7	6.587278							
10	8	6.959932							
11	9	6.79725							
12	10	6.684729							

This computes the mean and standard deviation of the two samples of 3.

11. From the Data tab, in the Analysis group select Data Analysis. Select Sampling. Click OK.

12. Leave the Input Range as **B3:B239**. In the Number of Samples text box, key **30.** In the Output Range text box, key **G3**. Click OK.

From the random weights in B3:B239, 30 were selected.

13. From the Data tab, in the Analysis group select Data Analysis. Select Sampling. Click OK.

14. Leave the Input Range as **B3:B239**. Leave the Number of Samples as **30**. In the Output Range text box, key **H3**. Click OK.

From the random weights in B3:B239, 30 more were selected.

15. In F33:F34, key **Mean** and **StdDev**, respectively.

16. In G33, key =**AVERAGE(G3:G32)**

17. In G34, key =**STDEV(G3:G32)**

18. Highlight **G33:G34**. Drag the lower right handle of G34 to H34.

This computes the mean and standard deviation of the two samples of 30.

19. Highlight **A9:A30**. (Column A will stop at Sample Number 28). From the Home tab in the Cells group, select Format. Under Visibility, select Hide & Unhide. Select Hide Rows.

This hides rows 9-30 and brings your mean and standard deviation of all 4 samples closer together so you can compare them.

	A	B	C	D	E	F	G	H	I
1	Sample	Birth			Sample	Sample	Sample	Sample	
2	Number	Weights			of 3	of 3	of 30	of 30	
3	1	7.403472			6.845856	7.04544	7.290466	6.476734	
4	2	7.337615			6.758911	6.922607	6.952859	7.098922	
5	3	6.692735			6.728874	7.45883	7.085119	7.012676	
6	4	6.8831		Mean	6.77788	7.142292	6.771342	7.255937	
7	5	6.934702		StdDev	0.060754	0.280925	6.119746	7.678632	
8	6	7.167506					6.393192	7.069464	
31	29	7.161848					7.067572	7.325329	
32	30	7.188481					7.316917	6.744359	
33	31	7.052134			Mean		7.026196	7.051699	
34	32	7.559373			StdDev		0.479805	0.376885	
35	33	6.925036							
36	34	7.038894							
37									

20. In C36:C37, key **% of diff mean** and **% of diff StdDev**, respectively.

21. In H36:H37, key **% of diff mean** and **% of diff StdDev**, respectively.

22. In E36, key **=ABS(E6-F6)/E6**

This computes the absolute (positive) value of the percent of difference between the two means.

23. In E37, key **=ABS(E7-F7)/E7**

24. In G36, key **=ABS(G33-H33)/G33**

25. In G37, key **=ABS(G34-H34)/G34**

This allows you to compare the means and standard deviations.

	A	B	C	D	E	F	G	H	I
1	Sample	Birth			Sample	Sample	Sample	Sample	
2	Number	Weights			of 3	of 3	of 30	of 30	
3	1	7.403472			6.845856	7.04544	7.290466	6.476734	
4	2	7.337615			6.758911	6.922607	6.952859	7.098922	
5	3	6.692735			6.728874	7.45883	7.085119	7.012676	
6	4	6.8831		Mean	6.77788	7.142292	6.771342	7.255937	
7	5	6.934702		StdDev	0.060754	0.280925	6.119746	7.678632	
8	6	7.167506					6.393192	7.069464	
31	29	7.161848					7.067572	7.325329	
32	30	7.188481					7.316917	6.744359	
33	31	7.052134				Mean	7.026196	7.051699	
34	32	7.559370				StdDev	0.479805	0.376885	
35	33	6.925036							
36	34	7.038894	% of diff mean		0.053765		0.00363	% of diff mean	
37			% of diff StdDev		3.623976		0.214504	% of diff StdDev	
38									

26. Highlight **E36:G37**. From the Home tab, in the Number group, select the Percent Style icon.

27. From the Home tab, in the Number group, select the Increase Decimal icon. Click one time.

This changes the format of the differences to percents with one place past the decimal.

	C	D	E	F	G	H	I	J	K
1			Sample	Sample	Sample	Sample			
2			of 3	of 3	of 30	of 30			
3			6.845856	7.04544	7.290466	6.476734			
4			6.758911	6.922607	6.952859	7.098922			
5			6.728874	7.45883	7.085119	7.012676			
6		Mean	6.77788	7.142292	6.771342	7.255937			
7		StdDev	0.060754	0.280925	6.119746	7.678632			
8					6.393192	7.069464			
31					7.067572	7.325329			
32					7.316917	6.744359			
33				Mean	7.026196	7.051699			
34				StdDev	0.479805	0.376885			
35									
36	% of diff mean		5.4%		0.4%	% of diff mean			
37	% of diff StdDev		362.4%		21.5%	% of diff StdDev			
38									

Each worksheet will be different. In the example above you can see that between the two samples of 3 each, the percent of difference in the means was 5.4% and the percent of difference in the standard deviation was 362.4%. Between the two samples of 30 each, the percent of difference in the means was only .4% and the percent of difference in the standard deviation was only 21.5%.

There was more difference in the means and standard deviation of the smaller samples than of the larger samples. Also in the two samples of 30, the means, 7.03 and 7.05 are much closer to the population mean of the birth weights (7.04). Every sample will be different, but in general the larger samples should have less variation.

If you wish to show the results of this exercise, you can print only the first page of your worksheet by doing the following:

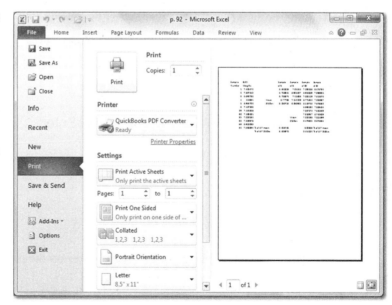

1. From the File Button, select Print.

2. From the Print dialog box, in the text box to the right of pages: key **1**.

3. In the to text box, key **1**.

4. Click on the Printer icon.

If you wish, save your file as **rand-1**. Close your file.

c. Plotting of Sample Means

Construct histograms using a very small sampling distribution of sample means and a larger sampling distribution of sample means.

1. On a new worksheet, enter the data as shown below.

	A	B	C	D	E	F	G	H	I
1	Sample	Sample Values			Sample				
2	Number	1	2	3	Mean	Class	Freq		
3	1								
4	2								
5	3								
6	4								
7	5								
8	6								
9	7								
10	8								
11	9								
12	10								
13	11								
14	12								
15									

2. Make B3 your active cell. Key **=NORM.INV(RAND(),7.04,.42)**. Press <Enter>.

3. Make B3 your active cell. Place your mouse arrow on the lower right handle of B3. Make sure you have a thick, black plus sign. Click your left mouse button twice, rapidly.

4. Highlight **B3:B14**. Place your mouse arrow on the lower right handle of B14. Drag B14 to C14:D14.

This generates random numbers.

5. In E3, key **=AVERAGE(B3:D3)**. Press <Enter>.

6. Using step 3, copy E3 to E4:E14.

This is the mean of each sample.

7. In F3 and F4, key **5.9** and **6.15**, respectively.

8. Highlight **F3:F4**. Place your mouse pointer on the lower right handle of F4. Drag to F5:F14.

This increases the weights in increments of .25 between 5.9 and 8.65.

9. Highlight **G3:G14**. With the range still highlighted, key **=FREQUENCY(E3:E14,F3:F14)** <u>DO NOT TOUCH THE <ENTER> KEY YET!</u>

10. After you have finished keying, hold down the <Shift> key and the <Ctrl> key together and at the same time touch the <Enter> key. The formula in the formula bar at the top of the worksheet should be inside curly brackets, { }.

This is called an *array*. An array links the data together and prevents the formula from being accidentally over-written.

Your worksheet should be similar to the one below. The numbers will be different but the format should be the same.

	A	B	C	D	E	F	G	H	I
1	Sample	Sample Values			Sample				
2	Number	1	2	3	Mean	Class	Freq		
3	1	7.002539	7.280273	7.187026	7.156613	5.9	0		
4	2	7.327805	6.956624	6.062287	6.782239	6.15	0		
5	3	6.172979	7.20566	7.690013	7.022884	6.4	0		
6	4	7.117397	7.202021	7.015982	7.1118	6.65	0		
7	5	7.360181	7.42049	6.095902	6.958858	6.9	2		
8	6	7.685653	6.674532	7.538569	7.299585	7.15	6		
9	7	6.769168	7.620385	6.497883	6.962478	7.4	3		
10	8	7.086487	7.031336	7.556749	7.224857	7.65	1		
11	9	7.742453	7.080808	7.38549	7.402917	7.9	0		
12	10	6.792978	7.117965	7.486402	7.132448	8.15	0		
13	11	7.325317	6.265432	6.596144	6.728964	8.4	0		
14	12	6.710974	6.930944	7.248558	6.963492	8.65	0		
15									

Touch the F9 function key on your keyboard. The numbers in the frequency column should change.

You will now plot the frequency distribution on a histogram.

11. Highlight **F3:G14**. From the Insert tab, in the Charts group, select Column. Select the 1st chart, Clustered Column.

12. From the Design tab, in the Chart Layouts group, click on the bottom down arrow. Select Layout 8.

13. From the Design tab, in the Data group choose Select Data. In the Select Data Source dialog box, under Legend Entries (Series), select, Series 1. Then select X Remove. (We don't want the class as part of the values) In the same Select Data Source dialog box, under Horizontal (Category) Axis Labels, click Edit. An Axis Labels dialog box will show. In the Axis label range box, key **=Sheet1!$F$3:$F$14**. Click OK. Click OK.

14. In your chart, click on the Chart Title. A box appears around it. Key **Mean Weights for Babies.** As you type the title shows in the equation box. Push <Enter>. The title is displayed in the chart. In the chart, click on the Vertical (Value) Axis Title. Key **Frequency.** Push <Enter>. In the chart, click on the Horizontal (Category) Axis Title. Key **Interval Weights**. Push <Enter>

15. From the Layout tab, in the Axes group, select Gridlines. Select Primary Horizontal Gridlines. Select Major Gridlines.

16. Point to the Horizontal (Category) Axis numbers at the bottom of the chart. Right click your mouse. Select Format Axis. In the Format Axis dialog box, under Axis Options, select the radio button for Specify internal unit. In the text box, key 2. Select Close.

17. Point to the Vertical (Value) Axis numbers at the left of the chart. Right click your mouse. Select Format Axis. In the Format Axis dialog box, under Axis Options, select the radio button for Maximum Fixed. In the text box, key 8. Select Close.

A condensed chart is displayed.

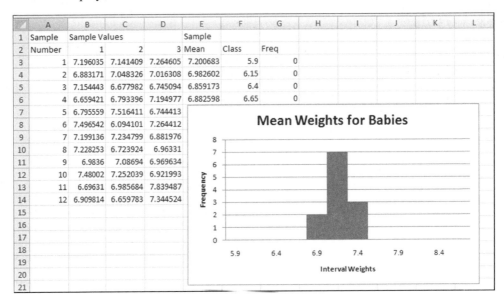

18. With the handles still on the chart, click and hold the left mouse button inside the Chart Area. A 4-way arrow will show in the chart. With your mouse button still depressed, drag your mouse and move your chart so the upper left corner of the chart is in cell H2. Move the right border to column M.

19. Click on your bottom scroll bar until you can see the columns for class and frequency and the chart all on the same screen.

Touch the F9 function key on your keyboard. The histogram will change according to the random weights selected.

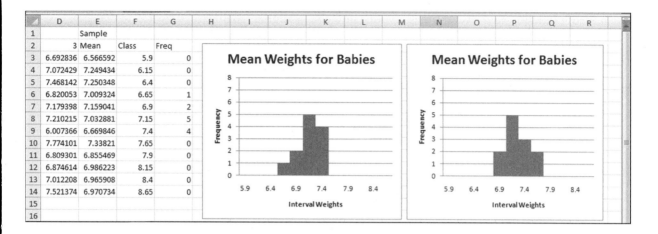

	D	E	F	G	H	I	J	K	L	M	N	O	P	Q	R
1		Sample													
2		3 Mean	Class	Freq											
3	6.692836	6.566592	5.9	0											
4	7.072429	7.249434	6.15	0											
5	7.468142	7.250348	6.4	0											
6	6.820053	7.009324	6.65	1											
7	7.179398	7.159041	6.9	2											
8	7.210215	7.032881	7.15	5											
9	6.007366	6.669846	7.4	4											
10	7.774101	7.33821	7.65	0											
11	6.809301	6.855469	7.9	0											
12	6.874614	6.986223	8.15	0											
13	7.012208	6.965908	8.4	0											
14	7.521374	6.970734	8.65	0											
15															
16															

You will have a variety of charts that may resemble a normal curve, or they may appear skewed. Compare your chart with the two sample charts shown above. As you touch the F9 key your chart will change. At times it may look very different from the above example, or very similar.

If you wish to show the results of this exercise, you can print only the first page of your worksheet by doing the following. Highlight **A1:D1**. From the Home tab, in the Cells group, select Format. Under Visibility, select Hide & Unhide. Select Hide Columns. This hides part of your worksheet so you can print more easily. From the File Button, select Print. From the Print dialog box, in the text box to the right of pages: key **1**. In the to text box, key **1**. Click on the Printer icon.

To unhide the columns, click your mouse on the row heading 1 so the whole row is highlighted. From the Home tab, in the Cells group, select Format. Under Visibility, select Hide & Unhide. Select Unhide Columns.

You will now insert additional columns so you can observe how the frequency of the means changes when there is a larger sample.

20. Highlight **C1:AC1**. As you move your mouse it will highlight the extra columns. From the Home tab, in the Cells group, select the down arrow next to Insert. Select Insert Sheet Columns.

This inserts extra columns between the existing columns so you will not have to re-enter the formulas for the mean and frequency.

21. Make B2 your active cell. From the Home tab, in the Editing group, place your cursor on the Fill icon. It shows as a down arrow. Select Series. From the Series dialog box, select Series in Rows. Select Type Linear. In the Step Value text box, key **1**. In the Stop Value text box, key **30**. Click OK.

22. Highlight **B3:B14**. Drag the lower right handle of B14 to C14:AC14.

Click on the bottom scroll bar until your histogram is visible

23. Point to the Vertical (Value) Axis numbers at the left of the chart. Right click your mouse. Select Format Axis. In the Format Axis dialog box, under Axis Options, select the radio button for Maximum Fixed. In the text box, key **12**. Select Close

Push the F9 function key several times. Notice how the histogram changes.

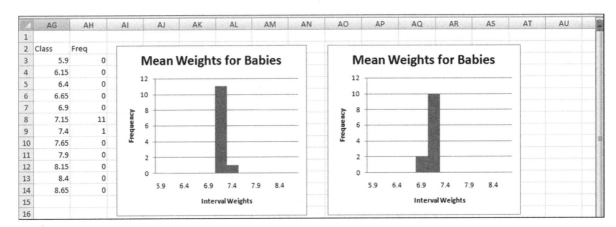

Compare your chart with the two sample charts shown above. Even though your chart changes, the bars are pretty much centered around the middle because taking the mean of several means reduces the amount of dispersion.

If you wish to show the results of this exercise, you can print only the first page of your worksheet by doing the following. Highlight **A1:AD1**. From the Home tab, in the Cells group, select Format. Under Visibility, select Hide & Unhide. Select Hide Columns. This hides part of your worksheet so you can print more easily. From the File Button, select Print. From the Print dialog box, in the text box to the right of pages: key **1**. In the to text box, key **1**. Click on the Printer icon.

If you wish save your worksheet as **rand-2**. Close your file.

Central Limits Theorem: Sampling From a Uniform Population

Example 2. A class of 32 statistics students were assigned to randomly select seven telephone numbers from a phone book. They were then asked to record the last digit of each phone number and find the mean of the seven numbers they recorded. This problem could illustrate the results of sampling from a uniform population if they created a histogram of the 32 sample means. It may look like the following example.

1. On a new worksheet, enter the data as shown.

	A	B	C	D	E	F	G	H	I	J	K
1	Sample	Data							Sample		
2	Number	1	2	3	4	5	6	7	Mean	Interval	Freq
3	1										
4											

2. Make A3 your active cell. From the Home tab, in the Editing group, place your cursor on the Fill icon. It shows as a **down arrow**. Select Series. From the Series dialog box, select Series in Columns. Select Type Linear. In the Step Value text box, key **1**. In the Stop Value text box, key **32**. Click OK.

3. Make B3 your active cell. Key =**RAND()*10**

4. Make B3 your active cell. Place your mouse arrow on the lower right handle of B3. Make sure you have a thick, black plus sign. Click your left mouse button twice, rapidly.

5. Highlight **B3:B34**. Place your mouse arrow on the lower right handle of B34. Drag B34 to C34:H34.

This generates random numbers.

6. While B3:H34 is still highlighted, from the Home tab, in the Number group, select the Decrease Decimal icon several times until all the figures appear as whole numbers.

7. Highlight **A1:H1**. From the Home tab, in the Cells group, select Format. Under Cell Size, select Column Width. In the Column Width text box, key **7**. Click OK.

This decreases the width of your worksheet making it easier to view.

8. In I3 key =**AVERAGE(B3:H3)**

9. Make I3 your active cell. Place your mouse arrow on the lower right handle of I3. Make sure you have a thick, black plus sign. Click your left mouse button twice, rapidly.

10. In J3:J4, key **2.0** and **2.4**, respectively.

11. Highlight **J3:J4**. Place your mouse arrow on the lower right handle of J4, Drag to J5:J18.

12. Highlight **K3:K18**. With the range still highlighted, key =**FREQUENCY(I3:I34,J3:J18)** <u>DO NOT TOUCH THE <ENTER> KEY YET!</u>

13. After you have finished keying, hold down the <Shift> key and the <Ctrl> key together and at the same time touch the <Enter> key. The formula in the formula bar at the top of the worksheet should be inside curly brackets, { }.

Touch the F9 function key on your keyboard. The numbers in the frequency column should change.

You will now plot the frequency distribution on a histogram.

14. Highlight **J3:K18**. From the Insert tab, in the Charts group, select Column. Select the 1st chart, Clustered Column.

15. From the Design tab, in the Chart Layouts group, click on the bottom down arrow. Select Layout 8.

16. From the Design tab, in the Data group choose Select Data. In the Select Data Source dialog box, under Legend Entries (Series), select, Series 1. Then select X Remove. (We don't want the class as part of the values) In the same Select Data Source dialog box, under Horizontal (Category) Axis Labels, click Edit. An Axis Labels dialog box will show. In the Axis label range box, key =**Sheet1!$J$3:$J$18**. Click OK. Click OK.

17. In your chart, click on the Chart Title. A box appears around it. Key **Uniform Sample.** Push <Enter>. In the chart, click on the Vertical (Value) Axis Title. Key **Frequency.** Push <Enter>. In the chart, click on the Horizontal (Category) Axis Title. Key **Sample Means.** Push <Enter>.

18. From the Layout tab, in the Axes group, select Gridlines. Select Primary Horizontal Gridlines. Select Major Gridlines.

19. Point to the Horizontal (Category) Axis numbers at the bottom of the chart. Right click your mouse. Select Format Axis. In the Format Axis dialog box, under Axis Options, select the radio button for Specify internal unit. In the text box, key **2.** Select Close.

20. Point to the Vertical (Value) Axis numbers at the left of the chart. Right click your mouse. Select Format Axis. In the Format Axis dialog box, under Axis Options, select the radio button for Maximum Fixed. In the text box, key **10.** Select Close.

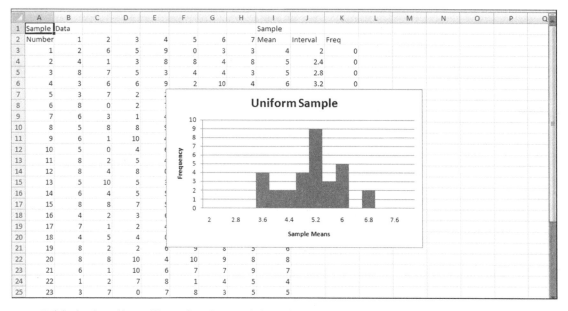

	Sample Data							Sample		
Number	1	2	3	4	5	6	7 Mean	Interval	Freq	
1	2	6	5	9	0	3	3	4	2	0
2	4	1	3	8	8	4	8	5	2.4	0
3	8	7	5	3	4	4	3	5	2.8	0
4	3	6	6	9	2	10	4	6	3.2	0
5	3	7	2							
6	8	0	2							
7	6	3	1							
8	5	8	8							
9	6	1	10							
10	5	0	4							
11	8	2	5							
12	8	4	8							
13	5	10	5							
14	6	4	5							
15	8	8	7							
16	4	2	3							
17	7	1	2							
18	4	5	4							
19	8	2	2	6	9	8	5	6		
20	8	8	10	4	10	9	8	8		
21	6	1	10	6	7	7	9	7		
22	1	2	7	8	1	4	5	4		
23	3	7	0	7	8	3	5	5		

21. With the handles still on the chart, click and hold the left mouse button inside the chart. A 4-way arrow will show in the chart. With your mouse button still depressed, drag your mouse and move your chart so the left corner of the chart is in cell L3.

22. Click on your bottom scroll bar until you can see the columns for Interval and Frequency and the chart all on the same screen.

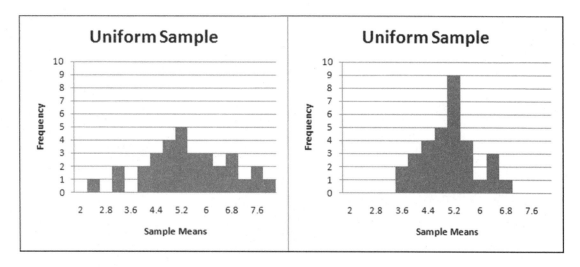

23. Click on the right handle of the chart. Drag the right line to the middle of column Q.

Touch the F9 function key on your keyboard and compare with the two sample charts shown above. The histogram will change according to the sample means selected. You will have a variety of charts but they should approximate a normal curve because of the central limits theorem.

If you wish to show the results of this exercise, you can print only the first page of your worksheet by doing the following. Highlight **A1:H1**. From the Home tab, in the Cells group, select Format. Under Visibility, select Hide & Unhide. Select Hide Columns. This hides part of your worksheet so you can print more easily. From the File Button, select Print. From the Print dialog box, in the text box to the right of pages: key **1**. In the to text box, key **1**. Click on the Printer icon.

If your wish, save your file as **rand-3**. Close your file.

Practice Exercises.

These exercises are in sampling, and every sample will be different. In general, larger samples will have less variation than smaller samples, and larger samples when graphed as a histogram will approximate a normal curve. There is no definitive answer.

8-1. The following table lists per capita personal income (in dollars) for each of 50 states.

1	Alabama	$27,795	18	Louisiana	27,581	35	Ohio	31,322
2	Alaska	34,454	19	Maine	30,566	36	Oklahoma	28,089
3	Arizona	28,442	20	Maryland	39,247	37	Oregon	29,971
4	Arkansas	25,725	21	Massachusetts	41,801	38	Pennsylvania	33,348
5	California	35,019	22	Michigan	31,954	39	Rhode Island	33,733
6	Colorado	36,063	23	Minnesota	35,861	40	South Carolina	27,172
7	Connecticut	45,398	24	Mississippi	24,650	41	South Dakota	30,856
8	Delaware	35,861	25	Missouri	30,608	42	Tennessee	30,005
9	Florida	31,455	26	Montana	26,857	43	Texas	30,222
10	Georgia	30,051	27	Nebraska	31,339	44	Utah	26,606
11	Hawaii	32,160	28	Nevada	33,405	45	Vermont	32,770
12	Idaho	27,098	29	New Hampshire	37,040	46	Virginia	35,477
13	Illinois	34,351	30	New Jersey	41,332	47	Washington	35,299
14	Indiana	30,094	31	New Mexico	26,191	48	West Virginia	25,872
15	Iowa	30,560	32	New York	38,228	49	Wisconsin	32,157
16	Kansas	30,811	33	North Carolina	29,246	50	Wyoming	34,306
17	Kentucky	27,709	34	North Dakota	31,398			

    a.   Generate a random frequency distribution of per capita personal income.

    b.   From the frequency distribution, select two small samples (sample size of 4) and two large samples (sample size of 40), and compare the means and standard deviations.

    c.   Construct histograms using a very small sampling distribution of sample means (sample size of 3) and a larger sampling distribution of sample means (sample size of 30). As you touch the F9 key to give you different charts, what do you notice between the charts of small sampling distributions and of larger sampling distributions?

8-2 Using the same data on per capita personal income found in problem 8-1, illustrate the central limit theorem. Use a sample size of 8 and create a histogram of the sample means.

CHAPTER
9
ESTIMATION AND CONFIDENCE INTERVALS

CHAPTER GOALS

After completing this chapter, you will be able to:

1. Define a point estimate.

2. Define level of confidence.

3. Use Excel to calculate a confidence interval for a population mean when the sample size is 30 or larger.

4. Use Excel to calculate a confidence interval for a proportion when the sample size is 30 or larger.

5. Use Excel to determine the sample size for estimating the population mean.

6. Use Excel to determine the sample size for estimating the population proportion.

Introduction

The previous chapter introduced **sampling** and the **central limit theorem**. We stressed that it is usually not feasible to inspect the entire population. Excel was used to show that the means of small samples have more dispersion or scatter than the means of large samples. We also used Excel to illustrate the **central limit theorem**. That is if all samples of a particular size are selected from any population, the sampling distribution of the sample mean is approximately a normal distribution. This approximation improves with larger samples.

In most situations we use sampling to find a **point estimate**, one number used to describe the population. Often only one number is not very useful if we do not know the dispersion or scatter. This chapter uses Excel to find a more informative estimate that presents a range of values in which the population value is expected to occur or a **confidence interval** of the population.

Point estimates are sample measures of central tendency such as mean, median and mode. Sample measures of dispersion such as variance and standard deviation are also point estimates.

Confidence intervals state the range within which a population parameter probably lies. The specified probability is called the *level of confidence*. A 95 percent confidence interval means that we have a 95 percent level of confidence that a similarly constructed interval will contain the parameter being estimated.

Frequently we need to determine the size of a sample. How many people should we contact to find the popularity of a political candidate or an idea? How many items do we examine to ensure product quality? This chapter uses Excel to calculate confidence intervals for population means and population proportions, and to determine sample size for estimating a mean or a proportion.

Confidence Intervals for a Population Mean

Example 1. The American Management Association wishes to have information on the mean income of store managers in the retail industry. A random sample of 256 managers reveals a sample mean of $45,420. The standard deviation of this population is $2050. What are the confidence limits at the 95% level of confidence?

The 99 percent confidence interval is $\overline{X} \pm z\dfrac{\sigma}{\sqrt{n}}$, where

$\overline{X}$ is the point estimate of the population mean.

The *z-value* depends on the level of confidence required.
     A 99 percent confidence results in a z-value of 2.58.
     A 95 percent confidence results in a z-value of 1.96.
     A 90 percent confidence results in a z-value of 1.645.

σ is the population standard deviation.

n is the number of samples.

     1. On a new worksheet enter the data as shown below.

	A	B	C	D	E	F	G	H	I
1	Confidence Interval-Mean								
2									
3	Mean=								
4	z=								
5	StdDev=								
6	n=								
7	Confidence Limits								
8	Lower	Upper							
9									

     2. In A9, type **=B3-B4*B5/SQRT(B6)**

     3. In B9, type **=B3+B4*B5/SQRT(B6)**

The cell contents for A9 and B9 display #DIV/0!. This is because you have not yet entered the variables.

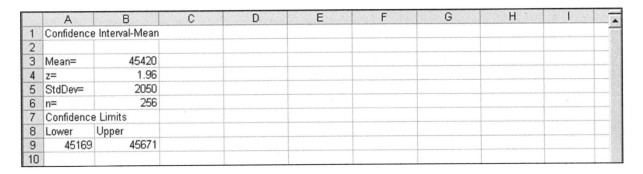

4. Save your file as **cnfdinv**.

All you need to do now is enter the variable numbers.

5. In B3:B6, enter respectively, **45420**, **1.96**, **2050**, and **256**.

6. Highlight cells A9 and B9. From the Home tab, in the Number group, use the Decrease Decimal button to round to a whole number.

	A	B	C	D	E	F	G	H	I	
1	Confidence Interval-Mean									
2										
3	Mean=	45420								
4	z=	1.96								
5	StdDev=	2050								
6	n=	256								
7	Confidence Limits									
8	Lower	Upper								
9	45169	45671								
10										

The lower and upper limits are displayed.

Confidence Interval for a Population Proportion

Example 2. The union representing the Bottle Blowers of America (BBA) is considering a proposal to merge with the Teamsters Union. According to BBA union bylaws, at least three-fourths of the union membership must approve any merger. A random sample of 2,000 current BBA members reveals 1,600 plan to vote for the merger proposal. Develop a 95 percent confidence interval for the population proportion?

The 95 percent confidence interval is $p \pm z \sqrt{\dfrac{p(1-p)}{n}}$, where:

p is the sample proportion.

The *z-value* depends on the level of confidence required, as in example 1.

n is the sample size.

1. On the same worksheet enter the data as shown in E1:F7.

	A	B	C	D	E	F	G
1	Confidence Interval-Mean				Confidence Interval-Proportion		
2							
3	Mean=	45420			Propor=		
4	z=	1.96			z=		
5	StdDev=	2050			n=		
6	n=	256			Confidence Limits		
7	Confidence Limits				Lower	Upper	
8	Lower	Upper					
9	45169	45671					
10							

2. In E8, key **=F3-F4*SQRT(F3*(1-F3)/F5)**

3. In F8, key **=F3+F4*SQRT(F3*(1-F3)/F5)**

The cell contents for E8 and F8 display #DIV/0!. This is because you have not yet entered the variables.

	A	B	C	D	E	F	G
1	Confidence Interval-Mean				Confidence Interval-Proportion		
2							
3	Mean=	45420			Propor=		
4	z=	1.96			z=		
5	StdDev=	2050			n=		
6	n=	256			Confidence Limits		
7	Confidence Limits				Lower	Upper	
8	Lower	Upper			#DIV/0!	#DIV/0!	
9	45169	45671					
10							

All you need to do now is enter the variable numbers.

    4. In F3, key **=1600/2000**

This is the proportion of the sample.

    5. In F4, key **1.96**

The confidence level is 99 percent.

    6. In F5, key **2000**

The lower and upper limits are displayed.

	A	B	C	D	E	F	G
1	Confidence Interval-Mean				Confidence Interval-Proportion		
2							
3	Mean=	45420			Propor=	0.8	
4	z=	1.96			z=	1.96	
5	StdDev=	2050			n=	2000	
6	n=	256			Confidence Limits		
7	Confidence Limits				Lower	Upper	
8	Lower	Upper			0.78247	0.81753	
9	45169	45671					
10							

If you wish, save your worksheet as **cnfdinv1**. Close your file.

Example 3. Determining a sample size for means.

The formula for determining a sample size for a mean is
$$n=\left[\frac{z\cdot\sigma}{E}\right]^2$$

The *z-value* depends on the level of confidence required.
    A 99 percent confidence results in a z-value of 2.58.
    A 95 percent confidence results in a z-value of 1.96.
    A 90 percent confidence results in a z-value of 1.645.

σ is the population standard deviation.

E is the maximum allowable error.

Problem: A **stu**dent in Public Administration wants to conduct a study to determine the mean amount members of city councils earn. The error in estimating the mean is to be less than $100 with a 95 percent level of confidence. The student found a report by the Department of Labor that reported a standard deviation of $1,000. What is the sample size?

1. On a new worksheet, in A1, key **Sample size for mean**.

2. In A3, key **z-value=**

3. in A4, key **StdDev=**

4. In A5, key **error=**

5. In A6 key **sample size=**

6. In A7, key **rounded=**

7. Highlight cell A6. From the Home tab, in the Cells group, click on the down arrow next to Format.

8. Under Cell Size, click on AutoFit Column Width. Column A widens for the text.

9. In B6, key **=((B3*B4)/B5)^2**

The contents of B6 will display #DIV/0!. It will change when you fill in the values.

	A	B	C	D	E	F	G	H	I
1	Sample size for mean								
2									
3	Z-value=								
4	StdDev=								
5	error=								
6	sample size=	#DIV/0!							
7	rounded=								
8									

10. In B3, key **1.96**, since the confidence required is 95 percent.

11. In B4, key **1000**, the estimated standard deviation.

12. In B5, key **100**, since the error is to be less than 100.

The sample size of 384.16 is displayed in B6.

13. In B7, key **=INT(B6+.99)** This rounds up the answer to the next whole number of 385.

14. Bold the contents of A1 and B7.

	A	B	C	D	E	F	G	H	I
1	Sample size for mean								
2									
3	Z-value=	1.96							
4	StdDev=	1000							
5	error=	100							
6	sample size=	384.16							
7	rounded=	**385**							
8									

Example 4. Determining a sample size for proportion.

The formula for determining a sample size for a proportion is $n = \pi(1-\pi)\left(\dfrac{z}{E}\right)^2$

The *z-value* depends on the level of confidence required, as in example 3.

π is the population proportion if known. If the proportion is not known, π is assigned a value of .5.

E is the margin of error in the proportion that is requested.

Problem: The study in the previous example also estimates the proportion of cities that have private refuse collectors. The student wants the margin of error to be within .10 of the population proportion, the desired level of confidence is 90 percent, and no estimate is available for the population proportion. What is the required sample size?

1. On the same worksheet as example 3, in cell A9, key **Sample size for proportion.**
2. In A11, key **z-value=**
3. In A12, key **PopPro=**
4. In A13, key **error=**
5. In A14, key **sample size=**
6. In B14, key **=B12*(1-B12)*(B11/B13)^2**
7. In A15, key **rounded=**

The contents of B14 will display #DIV/0!. It will change when you fill in the values.

8. In B11, key **1.645**, since the confidence required is 90 percent.
9. In B12, key **.5**, since the population proportion is not known.
10. In B13, key **.10**, since the error should not exceed 10 percent.

The sample size of 67.65063 is displayed in B14.

11. In B15 key, **=INT(B14+.99)** This rounds up the answer to the next whole number of 68.
12. Bold the contents of A9 and B15.

Chapter 9

	A	B	C	D	E	F	G	H	I
1	Sample size for mean								
2									
3	Z-value=	1.96							
4	StdDev=	1000							
5	error=	100							
6	sample size=	384.16							
7	rounded=	**385.00**							
8									
9	Sample size for proportion								
10									
11	Z-value=	1.645							
12	PopPro=	0.5							
13	error=	0.1							
14	sample size=	67.65063							
15	rounded=	**68.00**							
16									

If you wish, save your worksheet as **sampsize**.

You can do more than one problem on a worksheet. Just copy the formulas on another part of the worksheet. For example if you wanted to find another sample size for proportion, you would highlight A9:B15. From the **Home** tab, in the **Clipboard** group, you could click your mouse arrow on the **Copy** icon. You would make the cell active where you wanted the formula to be, for instance, E1, then you would click your mouse arrow on the **Paste** icon, and touch the <Enter> key. Be sure to identify each problem and bold the answer to identify it more easily.

Practice Exercises taken from textbook.

9-1. A random sample of 85 group leaders, supervisors, and similar personnel at General Motors revealed that, on the average, a person spent 6.5 years on the job before being promoted. The standard deviation of the sample was 1.7 years. Using the .95 degree of confidence, construct the confidence interval within which the population mean lies. (Textbook Problem 9-27)

9-2. There are 20,000 eligible voters in York County of South Carolina. A random sample of 500 York County voters revealed 350 plan to vote to return Louella Miller to the state senate. Construct a 99 percent confidence interval for the proportion of voters in the county who plan to vote for Ms. Miller. From this sample information can you confirm she will be re-elected? (Textbook Problem 9-45)

9-3. We want to estimate the population mean within 5, with a 99 percent level of confidence. The population standard deviation is estimated to be 15. How large a sample is required?
(Textbook Problem 9-20)

9-4. The estimate of the population proportion is to be within plus or minus .10, with a 99 percent level of confidence. The best estimate of the population proportion is .45. How large a sample is required?
(Textbook Problem 9-22)

CHAPTER
10
ONE-SAMPLE TESTS OF HYPOTHESIS

CHAPTER GOALS

After completing this chapter, you will be able to:

1. Define a hypothesis and hypothesis testing.

2. Use Excel to conduct a z-test of hypothesis about a population mean with a known population standard deviation.

3. Use Excel to conduct a t-test of hypothesis for a population mean, when the population standard deviation is unknown.

4. Use Excel to conduct a z-test of hypothesis about a population proportion.

Introduction

Chapter 8 and 9 dealt with a segment of statistical inference called estimation. This chapter will deal with a method of testing those estimations. Hypothesis testing is a procedure based on sample evidence and probability theory. It is used to determine whether the hypothesis is a reasonable statement and should not be rejected, or is unreasonable and should be rejected.

The terms, **hypothesis testing** and **testing a hypothesis** are used interchangeably. Hypothesis testing starts with a statement, or assumption about a population parameter. We then analyze the differences between the results actually observed and the results we would expect to obtain if some underlying hypothesis were actually true. When we do this we also evaluate the risks involved in making these decisions based on sample information and the interrelationship of these risks based on sample size. In this chapter and several of the following chapters, numerous hypothesis testing procedures will be presented that are frequently employed in the analysis of data obtained from studies and experiments designed under a variety of conditions. The following statements could be tested using hypothesis techniques:

- A college dean says the mean age of students is 25.

- A medical center study shows a new procedure is more than 82 percent successful.

- Q Lube claims the average waiting time for their customers is less than 17 minutes.

Steps in hypothesis testing:

These five steps in hypothesis testing will help you solve a wide variety of hypothesis problems, not just those using a z test for large samples. The five step process provides a similar format and a thread of continuity that can be helpful in recognizing different statistical tests and knowing which test to apply different situations.

1. **State the null and alternative hypothesis** using either formulas or words.
The Null Hypothesis (H_o) is the statement of "no change" or significant difference.

   The Alternative Hypothesis (H_1) is the statement that there is a significant difference. When direction is stated it is a one-directional test (one-tailed). When direction is not stated it is a two-directional test (two-tailed).

2. **Select the level of significance** or the probability that the null hypothesis is rejected when, in fact, it is true.

3. **Select the test statistic** you will be using: the z test, t test, f test, Chi Square test, etc.

4. **Formulate the decision rule**. Using a picture or curve that estimates the distribution you are testing, show the critical value if you are performing a one-directional test or the upper and lower critical values if you are performing a two-directional test.

5. **Make a Decision**. State the results of the hypothesis test in terms of the question using complete sentences and examples.

In Chapter 10 you will be using formulas to solve problems. You will also need to build an Excel worksheet before completing a hypothesis test. In building this worksheet, it is often helpful to use names in a formula instead of cell references. The following exercise will give you some experience naming cells and using the names in a formula:

$$\mu = \frac{\Sigma X}{N}$$

Remember, to switch to formula view, hold the control key down while tapping the tilde key. You may have to adjust the column width to be able to view the entire formula. Or from the Formulas tab, in the Formula Auditing group, choose Show Formulas.

Example 1. There are 6 students in a computer class. Their test scores were 92, 96, 61, 86, 79, and 84. What is the mean test grade?

The formula for finding the population mean is sum of all the values in the population divided by the number of values in the population.

1. On a new worksheet, enter the following as shown.

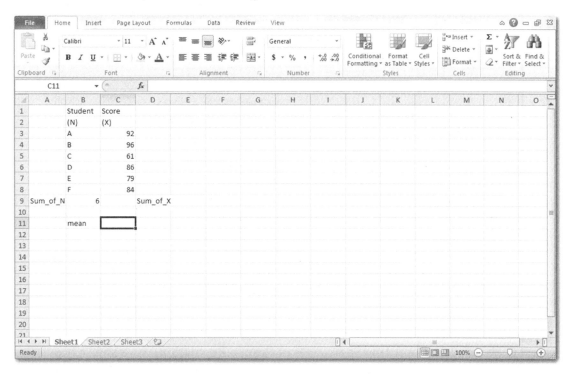

2. Highlight **B3:B8**. From the Home tab, in the Alignment group, click on the Align Right button.

3. Highlight **C3:C8**. From the Home tab, in the Editing group, click on the AutoSum button.

The sum of X (498) is displayed in cell C9.

4. Highlight **A9:B9**. From the Formulas tab, in the Defined Names group, select Create from Selection. Select the check box for Left Column. Click OK.

Notice that when B9 is selected as the active cell, the name of the cell (Sum_of_N) shows in the Name box in the upper left corner.

5. Highlight **C9:D9**. From the Formulas tab, in the Defined Names group, select Create from Selection. Select the check box for Right Column. Click on OK.

Notice that when C9 is selected as the active cell, the name of the cell (Sum_of_X) shows in the Name box in the upper left corner.

6. Make C11 your active cell. Key **=Sum_of_X/Sum_of_N**. Touch <Enter>. The population mean (83) is displayed.

You could have keyed the formula =C9/B9, but you used the names of those cells instead.

Notice that when C11 is selected as the active cell, the formula =Sum_of_X/Sum_of_N shows in the Formula bar at the top of the worksheet.

C11	▼	=	=Sum_of_X/Sum_of_N						
	A	B	C	D	E	F	G	H	I
1		Student	Score						
2		(N)	(X)						
3		A	92						
4		B	96						
5		C	61						
6		D	86						
7		E	79						
8		F	84						
9	Sum_of_N	6	498 Sum_of_X						
10									
11		mean	83						
12									

The previous exercise was to prepare you for creating formulas using names of cells, which is often easier to visualize than using just the cell references.

You will create a worksheet for hypothesis testing of large samples. It can be used for one left-tail, one right-tail, or a two-tailed hypothesis test. After the worksheet is created, you will be able to enter the input data. The worksheet will compute the results for all three kinds of hypothesis tests. You must then decide which one is needed for your test.

A Test of Hypothesis About One Sample Mean From a Population with a known population standard deviation.

The worksheet you create will include formulas used in your textbook. The symbols will often be referred to as names. The formula for finding the test statistic z is $z = \dfrac{\overline{X} - \mu}{\sigma / \sqrt{n}}$.

$\overline{X}$ is the sample mean. It will be referred to as SaMean.

μ is the hypothesis mean. It will be referred to as HoMean.

σ is the population standard deviation. It will be referred to as StdDev.

n is the sample size. It will be referred to as n.

Example 2 Creating a worksheet for testing of normal hypothesis of a one sample (population) mean.

1. On a new worksheet, enter the following data as shown.

2. Widen column A by double clicking your mouse arrow between column headings A and B.

3. Highlight **A5:A9**. From the Home tab, in the Alignment group, click on the Align Right button.

4. Right Align cell A11. Right align Cells A13:A15. Right align Cells A17:A19. Right align cells A21:A23.

	A	B	C	D	E	F	G	H
1	Test of Normal Hypotheses:							
2	One Sample Mean							
3								
4	Input Data							
5	HoMean							
6	SaMean							
7	n							
8	StdDev							
9	Alpha							
10	Calculated Value							
11	z							
12	Test for Left-Tail							
13	LftCrt_zVal							
14	Conclusion							
15	p-value							
16	Test for Right-Tail							
17	RtCrt_zVal							
18	Conclusion							
19	p-value							
20	Test for Two-Tail							
21	AbsCrt_zVal							
22	Conclusion							
23	p-value							

5. Highlight **A5:B9**. From the Formulas tab, in the Defined Names group, select Create from Selection. Select the check box for Left Column. Click on OK. The cells B5:B9 have names as well as cell references.

6. Highlight **A11:B11**. Use the same method from step 5 to create a name.

7. Use step 5 to create a name for A13:B13, A17:B17, and A21:B21

8. Make B11 your active cell. Key **=(SaMean-HoMean)/(StdDev/SQRT(n))** Touch <Enter>.

This is the formula for finding z.

The output result in cell B11 shows #DIV/0! This is because none of the input data have values yet (so the formula is trying to divide by 0). When you start entering the input data, the formulas will generate the correct output.

9. Make B13 your active cell. Key =**NORM.S.INV(Alpha)** Touch <Enter>.

This is the formula for finding the left critical value of z. There is no value for the output because there has been no input data.

As you key the remaining formulas, there will be no output value for any of the cells. The values will be obtained when the input data is entered later.

After each formula is completed, touch the <Enter> key. If you make a mistake and have already entered the formula, double click your mouse arrow on the cell and you will be able to edit the cell without rekeying the entire contents.

10. Make B17 your active cell. Key **=-NORM.S.INV(Alpha)**

This is the formula for finding the right critical value of z.

11. Make B21 your active cell. Key **=ABS(NORM.S.INV(Alpha/2))**

This is the formula for finding the critical value of z on a two-tailed test.

12. Make B14 your active cell. Key **=If(z<LftCrt_zVal, "Reject Ho", "Do Not Reject Ho")**

This is the decision to reject or not to reject the null hypothesis of a left-tail test. If the test statistic of z is less than the left critical z value, then the hypothesis is rejected. Otherwise do not reject the null hypothesis.

13. Make B18 your active cell. Key **=If (z>RtCrt_zVal, "Reject Ho", "Do Not Reject Ho")**

This is the decision to reject or not to reject the null hypothesis of a right-tail test. If the test statistic of z is greater than the right critical z value, then the hypothesis is rejected. Otherwise do not reject the null hypothesis.

14. Make B22 your active cell. Key **=If (OR(z<-AbsCrt_zVal, z>AbsCrt_zVal), "Reject Ho", "Do Not Reject Ho")**

This is a decision to reject or not to reject the null hypothesis of a two-tailed test.

If the test statistic of z is less than the negative critical z value *or* if the test statistic of z is greater than the critical z value, then reject the hypothesis. Otherwise do not reject the hypothesis.

You now need to enter the formula for the p-value for each of the three tests.

15. Make B15 your active cell. Key **=NORM.S.DIST(z,1)**

16. Make B19 your active cell. Key **=1-NORM.S.DIST(z,1)**

17. Make B23 your active cell. Key **=If(z>0,2*(1-NORM.S.DIST(z,1)),2*NORM.S.DIST(z,1))**

NOTE: As you work your problems, the answers may differ slightly from the textbook since Excel does not round z and t values. This should <u>not</u> affect the conclusion on whether or not to reject the hypothesis.

As you are entering the formulas, your worksheet will display the cell contents as shown below. (Toggle to Formula View with the control and tilde key). You can also use the **Formulas** tab. In the **Formula Auditing** group, Choose **Show Formulas**. Double click the left mouse button between columns B & C to see the whole formula. Click the Undo icon to decrease the column width. Toggle back to Regular View with the tilde key or click on **Show Formulas** again.

	A	B
1	Test of Normal Hypotheses:	
2	One Sample Mean	
3		
4	Input Data	
5	HoMean	
6	SaMean	
7	n	
8	StdDev	
9	Alpha	
10	Calculated Value	
11	z	=(SaMean-HoMean)/(StdDev/SQRT(n))
12	Test for Left-Tail	
13	LftCrt_zVal	=NORM.S.INV(Alpha)
14	Conclusion	=IF(z<LftCrt_zVal, "Reject Ho","Do Not Reject Ho")
15	p-value	=NORM.S.DIST(z,1)
16	Test for Right-Tail	
17	RtCrt_zVal	=-NORM.S.INV(Alpha)
18	Conclusion	=IF(z>RtCrt_zVal, "Reject Ho", "Do Not Reject Ho")
19	p-value	=1-NORM.S.DIST(z,1)
20	Test for Two-Tail	
21	AbsCrt_zVal	=ABS(NORM.S.INV(Alpha/2))
22	Conclusion	=IF(OR(z<-AbsCrt_zVal, z>AbsCrt_zVal), "Reject Ho", "Do Not Reject Ho")
23	p-value	=IF(z>0,2*(1-NORM.S.DIST(z,1)),2*NORM.S.DIST(z,1))
24		

After you have finished entering all the formulas, your worksheet will appear as shown below.

	A	B
1	Test of Normal Hypotheses:	
2	One Sample Mean	
3		
4	Input Data	
5	HoMean	
6	SaMean	
7	n	
8	StdDev	
9	Alpha	
10	Calculated Value	
11	z	#DIV/0!
12	Test for Left-Tail	
13	LftCrt_zVal	#NUM!
14	Conclusion	#DIV/0!
15	p-value	#DIV/0!
16	Test for Right-Tail	
17	RtCrt_zVal	#NUM!
18	Conclusion	#DIV/0!
19	p-value	#DIV/0!
20	Test for Two-Tail	
21	AbsCrt_zVal	#NUM!
22	Conclusion	#DIV/0!
23	p-value	#DIV/0!
24		

Save a copy of this worksheet so you can enter data into the input cells and not have to recreate the worksheet each time. Save as **1sa-mean.**

Example 3. Heinz, a manufacturer of ketchup, uses a particular machine to dispense 16 ounces of its ketchup into containers. From many years of experience with the particular dispensing machine, Heinz knows the amount of product in each container follows the normal distribution with a mean of 16 ounces and a standard deviation of 0.15 ounce. A sample of 50 containers filled last hour revealed the mean amount per container was 16.017 ounces. Does this evidence suggest that the mean amount dispensed is different from 16 ounces?

1. Open the file **1sa-mean** if it is not already active.

2. In cells B5:B9, enter the input data in the appropriate cells, as shown.

	A	B	C
1	Test of Normal Hypotheses		
2	One Sample Mean		
3			
4	Input Data		
5	HoMean	16	
6	SaMean	16.017	
7	n	50	
8	StdDev	0.15	
9	Alpha	0.05	
10			

The values in the output cells have automatically changed to reflect the input data.

B22		f_x	=IF(OR(z<-AbsCrt_zVal,z>AbsCrt_zVal), "Reject Ho", "Do Not Reject Ho")						
	A	B	C	D	E	F	G	H	I
1	Test of Normal Hypotheses								
2	One Sample Mean								
3									
4	Input Data								
5	HoMean	16							
6	SaMean	16.017							
7	n	50							
8	StdDev	0.15							
9	Alpha	0.05							
10	Calculated Value								
11	z	0.801388							
12	Test for Left-Tail								
13	LftCrt_zVal	-1.64485							
14	Conclusion	Do Not Reject Ho							
15	p-value	0.788546							
16	Test for Right-Tail								
17	RtCrt_zVal	1.644854							
18	Conclusion	Do Not Reject Ho							
19	p-value	0.211454							
20	Test for Two-Tail								
21	AbsCrt_zVal	1.959964							
22	Conclusion	Do Not Reject Ho							
23	p-value	0.422907							
24									

You can then interpret the results. Since the calculated value for z of .801388 is in between a plus or minus 1.959964, we do not reject the null hypotheses. The rejection area is the area outside ± the absolute value of z.

We cannot conclude the mean amount dispensed is different from 16.0 ounces. The p-value tells you that you have a .422907 chance of rejecting a true null hypothesis (a type one error).

If you wish, save your worksheet as **example3**. Close your file.

A Test of Hypothesis About a Population Mean: Population Standard Deviation Unknown

If the standard deviation is unknown, the z distribution is not appropriate. In this case, the **t distribution**, is used as the test statistic.

The formula for a population t test is: $t = \dfrac{\overline{X} - \mu}{s / \sqrt{n}}$

$\overline{X}$ is the mean of the sample. It will be referred to as SaMean.

μ is the hypothesized population mean. It will be referred to as HoMean.

s is the standard deviation of the sample. It will be referred to as StdDev.

n is the number of observations in the sample. It will be referred to as n.

The decision to reject or not to reject the hypothesis (the t test) is very similar to the decision using the z test.

You will rename some cells, edit the formulas of some cells, and re-key the formulas in other cells. The formula for t tests requires the use of the degrees of freedom, df.

df is found by the formula df = n-1.

Example 4. Creating a worksheet for testing a population mean, population standard deviation unknown.

1. Open **1sa-mean**.

2. Make A1 your active cell. Key **Test for Population Mean**.

3. Make A2 your active cell. Key **Population Standard Deviation Unknown**.

4. Make A11 your active cell. From the Home tab, in the Cells group, select the down arrow next to Insert. Select Insert Sheet Rows.

The variables in A5:A9 remain the same, however some are computed differently.

5. Make B6 your active cell. Key =**AVERAGE(Sample)**. (Don't forget to touch the <Enter> key after entering each cell's contents.)

This computes the mean of your sample data, which you will enter later.

6. Make B8 your active cell. Key =**STDEV(Sample)**

This computes the standard deviation of your sample data, which you will enter later.

7. In cell A11, key **df**

8. Right align A11.

9. Highlight **A11:B11.** From the Formulas tab, in the Defined Names group, select Create from Selection. Select <u>L</u>eft Column. Click OK.

10. Make B11 your active cell. Key =**n-1**

This computes the degrees of freedom.

11. In A12, key **t**

12. Highlight **A12:B12**. Repeat the instructions in step 9 for creating a name.

You will notice that when B12 is your active cell, the name of the cell (t) shows in the name box in the upper left corner. B12 used to have the name z. You have renamed the cell, *t*.

13. Make A14 your active cell. Double click the left mouse button.

A gray shadow box appears around the cell. The cell can now be edited.

14. Use the arrow key to move the flashing vertical bar to the left of the letter z. Touch the <delete> key once. Key the letter **t**. (Remember to touch the <Enter> key when you are finished with editing).

Cell A14 should now read, LftCrt_tVal.

15. Make B14 your active cell. Key =**T.INV(Alpha,df)**

This replaces the old formula for LftCrt_zVal with the new formula for LftCrt_tVal.

16. Highlight **A14:B14**. Use the instructions in step 9 for creating a name.

17. Make B15 your active cell. Double click the left mouse button to edit the cell. Using your arrow keys to move the flashing vertical bar, delete the letter z both times and replace with the letter **t**.

Cell B15 should now read, =IF(t<LftCrt_tVal, "Reject Ho", "Do Not Reject Ho")

18. Make B16 your active cell. Key =**IF(t>0,T.DIST(t,df,1),1-T.DIST(ABS(t),df,1))**

This replaces the old formula for *p* with the new formula using the t test.

You will continue to edit some cell contents and rekey others.

19. Make A18 your active cell. Double click to edit the cell. Replace the letter z with the letter **t**.

Cell A18 should now read RtCrt_tVal.

20. Make B18 your active cell. Key =**-T.INV(Alpha,df)**

21. Highlight **A18:B18**. Use the instructions in step 9 for creating a name.

22. Make B19 your active cell. Double click to edit the cell. Delete the letter z both times and replace with the letter **t**.

Cell B19 should now read, =If(t>RtCrt_tVal, "Reject Ho", "Do Not Reject Ho")

23. Make B20 your active cell. Key **=IF(t>0, T.DIST.RT(t,df),1-T.DIST.RT(ABS(t),df))**

24. Make A22 your active cell. Double click to edit the cell. Replace the letter z with the letter **t**.

Cell A22 should now read, AbsCrt_tVal.

25. Make B22 your active cell. Key **=T.INV.2T(Alpha, df)**

26. Highlight **A22:B22**. Use the instructions in step 9 for creating a name.

27. Make B23 your active cell. Double click to edit the cell. Delete the letter z each time and replace with the letter **t**. There should be four.

Cell B23 should now read, = IF(OR(t<-AbsCrt_tVal,t>AbsCrt_tVal), "Reject Ho", "Do not Reject Ho")

28. Make B24 your active cell. Key **=T.DIST.2T(ABS(t),df)**

After you have finished editing, and re-keying the worksheet, it should have the cell contents as shown below.

⊿	A	B	C	D	E	F	G	H	I
1	Test for Population Mean								
2	Population Standard Deviation Unknown								
3									
4	Input Data								
5	HoMean								
6	SaMean	=AVERAGE(Sample)							
7	n								
8	StdDev	=STDEV(Sample)							
9	Alpha								
10	Calculated Value								
11	df	-1							
12	t	=(SaMean-HoMean)/(StdDev/SQRT(n))							
13	Test for Left-Tail								
14	LftCrt_tVal	=T.INV(Alpha,df)							
15	Conclusion	=IF(t<LftCrt_tVal, "Reject Ho","Do Not Reject Ho")							
16	p-value	=IF(t>0,T.DIST(t,df,1),1-T.DIST(ABS(t),df,1))							
17	Test for Right-Tail								
18	RtCrt_tVal	=-T.INV(Alpha,df)							
19	Conclusion	=IF(t>RtCrt_tVal, "Reject Ho", "Do Not Reject Ho")							
20	p-value	=IF(t>0,T.DIST.RT(t,df),1-T.DIST.RT(ABS(t),df))							
21	Test for Two-Tail								
22	AbsCrt_tVal	=T.INV.2T(Alpha,df)							
23	Conclusion	=IF(OR(t<-AbsCrt_tVal, t>AbsCrt_tVal), "Reject Ho", "Do Not Reject Ho")							
24	p-value	=T.DIST.2T(ABS(t),df)							
25									

The worksheet should appear as shown below.

	A	B	C
1	Test for Population Mean		
2	Population Standard Deviation Unknown		
3			
4	Input Data		
5	HoMean		
6	SaMean	#NAME?	
7	n		
8	StdDev	#NAME?	
9	Alpha		
10	Calculated Value		
11	df	-1	
12	t	#NAME?	
13	Test for Left-Tail		
14	LftCrt_tVal	#NUM!	
15	Conclusion	#NAME?	
16	p-value	#NAME?	
17	Test for Right-Tail		
18	RtCrt_tVal	#NUM!	
19	Conclusion	#NAME?	
20	p-value	#NAME?	
21	Test for Two-Tail		
22	AbsCrt_tVal	#NUM!	
23	Conclusion	#NAME?	
24	p-value	#NAME?	
25			

Save this worksheet as **t-tst1mn**.

Chapter 10

Example 5. A machine is set to fill a small bottle with 9.0 grams of medicine. A sample of eight bottles revealed the following amounts (grams) in each bottle: 9.2, 8.7, 8.9, 8.6, 8.8, 8.5, 8.7, and 9.0. At the .01 significance level, can we conclude that the mean weight is less than 9.0 grams?

1. Open the file **t-tst1mn**, if it is not already open.

2. Make D1 your active cell. Key **Sample**.

Don't forget to touch the **<Enter>** key after entering the contents of each cell.

3. In D2:D9, key in the sample weights as shown below.

	A	B	C	D	E
1	Test for Population Mean			Sample	
2	Population Standard Deviation Unknown			9.2	
3				8.7	
4	Input Data			8.9	
5		HoMean		8.6	
6		SaMean	#NAME?	8.8	
7		n		8.5	
8		StdDev	#NAME?	8.7	
9		Alpha		9	
10					

4. Highlight **D1:D9**. From the **Formulas** tab, in the **Defined Names** group, select **Create from Selection**. Select **Top Row**. Click **OK**.

This gives the sample weights a name (Sample), so you can use them in the formulas you created for SaMean and StdDev.

5. Enter the remaining data in cells B5, B7, and B9 as shown below.

df		fx =n-1			
	A	B	C	D	E
1	Test for Population Mean			Sample	
2	Population Standard Deviation Unknown			9.2	
3				8.7	
4	Input Data			8.9	
5		HoMean	9	8.6	
6		SaMean	8.8	8.8	
7		n	8	8.5	
8		StdDev	0.226779	8.7	
9		Alpha	0.01	9	
10	Calculated Value				
11		df	7		
12					

After you are through entering the formulas and data, the values in the output cells have automatically changed to reflect the input data.

	B15	▼	f_x	=IF(t<LftCrt_tVal, "Reject Ho", "Do Not Reject Ho")			
	A	B	C	D	E	F	G
1	Test for Population Mean			Sample			
2	Population Standard Deviation Unkown			9.2			
3				8.7			
4	Input Data			8.9			
5	HoMean	9		8.6			
6	SaMean	8.8		8.8			
7	n	8		8.5			
8	StdDev	0.226779		8.7			
9	Alpha	0.01		9			
10	Calculated Value						
11	df	7					
12	t	-2.49444					
13	Test for Left-Tail						
14	LftCrt_tVal	-2.99795					
15	Conclusion	Do Not Reject Ho					
16	p-value	0.020664					
17	Test for Right-Tail						
18	RtCrt_tVal	2.997952					
19	Conclusion	Do Not Reject Ho					
20	p-value	0.979336					
21	Test for Two-Tail						
22	AbsCrt_tVal	3.499483					
23	Conclusion	Do Not Reject Ho					
24	p-value	0.041327					
25							

You can now interpret the results. Accept the H_0. At the .01 significance the mean weight of the small bottles of medicine is not less than 9.0 grams.

If you wish, save your file as **ex5t-tst**. Close your file.

A Test of Hypothesis About a Single Proportion

In the last exercise you created a worksheet used to conduct a test of hypothesis about small sample population means. You will again make some changes to a previously created worksheet. This worksheet will then be used to test a hypothesis about a single proportion.

The formula for finding z is
$$z = \frac{p - \pi}{\sqrt{\dfrac{\pi(1 - \pi)}{n}}}$$

p is the proportion in the sample possessing the trait. It will be referred to as p.

π is the hypothesized population proportion. It will be referred to as pi.

n is the size of the sample. It will be referred to as n.

Example 6. Creating a worksheet for testing of hypothesis about a single proportion.

1. Retrieve the file **1sa-mean**.

2. Make A2 your active cell. Key **Single Proportion.**

3. Highlight **A5:A8**. From the Home tab, in the Cells group, select the down arrow next to Delete. Select Delete Sheet Rows.

This will delete the contents of the rows and the names of the cells that were created.

4. Highlight **A5:A7**. From Home tab, in the Cells group, select the down arrow next to Insert. Select Insert Sheet Rows.

This will give you blank rows to insert your input data.

5. In A5:A7, key the input variables, as shown below.

	A	B	C	D	E	F	G	H
1	Test of Normal Hypotheses:							
2	Single Proportion							
3								
4	Input Data							
5	p							
6	pi							
7	n							
8	Alpha							
9	Calculated Value							
10	z	#REF!						
11								

6. Highlight **A5:A7**. From the Home tab, in the Alignment group, select the Align Right icon.

7. Highlight **A5:B7**. From the Formulas tab, in the Defined Names group, select Create from Selection. Select <u>L</u>eft Column. Click OK. Select <u>Y</u>es, for Replace existing definition of 'n'?

Excel remembers *n* was used in an earlier worksheet. You are redefining *n*.

8. Make B10 your active cell. You will key the new formula for z. As you key, the previous formula for z will be replaced. Key **=(p-pi)/SQRT(pi*(1-pi)/n)**

	z		=	=(p-pi)/SQRT(pi*(1-pi)/n)						
	A	B	C	D	E	F	G	H		
1	Test of Normal Hypotheses:									
2	Single Proportion									
3										
4	Input Data									
5	p									
6	pi									
7	n									
8	Alpha									
9	Calculated Value									
10	z	#DIV/0!								
11	Test for Left-Tail									
12	LftCrt_zVal	#NUM!								
13	Conclusion	#DIV/0!								
14	p-value	#DIV/0!								
15										

Save the worksheet as **1-propor**.

Example 7. A recent insurance industry report indicated that 40 percent of those persons involved in minor traffic accidents this year have been involved in at least one other traffic accident in the last five years. An advisory group decided to investigate this claim believing it was too large. A sample of 200 traffic accidents this year showed 74 persons were also involved in another accident within the last five years. Use the .01 significance level to test this claim.

1. Open the file **1-propor** if it is not already active.

2. In cell B5, key = **74/200.**

By keying in the equation = 74/200, you are computing the sample proportion.

3. In B6:B8, enter the input data in the appropriate cells as shown below.

	p	▼		ƒx =74/200	
		A		B	C
1	Test of Normal Hypotheses:				
2	Single Proportion				
3					
4	Input Data				
5			p	0.37	
6			pi	0.4	
7			n	200	
8			Alpha	0.01	
9					

The values in the output cells have automatically changed to reflect the input data.

	B13	▼	ƒx	=IF(z<LftCrt_zVal, "Reject Ho","Do Not Reject Ho")			
	A	B	C	D	E	F	G
1	Test of Normal Hypotheses:						
2	Single Proportion						
3							
4	Input Data						
5	p	0.37					
6	pi	0.4					
7	n	200					
8	Alpha	0.01					
9	Calculated Value						
10	z	-0.86603					
11	Test for Left-Tail						
12	LftCrt_zVal	-2.32635					
13	Conclusion	Do Not Reject Ho					
14	p-value	0.193238					
15	Test for Right-Tail						
16	RtCrt_zVal	2.326348					
17	Conclusion	Do Not Reject Ho					
18	p-value	0.806762					
19	Test for Two-Tail						
20	AbsCrt_zVal	2.575829					
21	Conclusion	Do Not Reject Ho					
22	p-value	0.386476					
23							

You can now interpret the results. Since the calculated value for z of -0.86603 is greater than –2.32635, we accept the null hypothesis.

At least forty percent of those persons involved in minor traffic accidents this year have been involved in at least one other traffic accident in the last five years. The p-value shows that you have a .193238 chance of rejecting a true null hypothesis (a type one error) which is much higher than .01.

If you wish, save your worksheet as **example7**. Close your file.

Practice Exercises taken from textbook.

In addition to showing your printout, state the results of the hypothesis test in terms of the question using complete sentences and examples.

10-1. The waiting time for customers at MacBurger restaurant follows a normal distribution with a mean of 3 minutes and a standard deviation of 1 minute. The quality-assurance department found in a sample of 50 customers at the Warren Road MacBurger that the mean waiting time was 2.75 minutes. At the .05 significance level, can we say that the mean waiting time is less than 3 minutes at the Warren Road store? (Textbook Problem 10-6)

10-2. A new weight-watching company, Weight Reducers International, advertises that those who join will lose, on the average, 10 pounds the first two weeks with a standard deviation of 2.8 pounds. A random sample of 50 people who joined the new weight reduction program revealed the mean loss to be 9 pounds. At the .05 level of significance, can we conclude that those joining Weight Reducers on average will lose less than 10 pounds? Determine the p-value. (Textbook Problem 10-29)

10-3. According to a recent survey Americans get a mean of 7 hours sleep per night. A random sample of 50 students at West Virginia University revealed the mean number of hours slept last night was 6 hours and 48 minutes (6.8 hours). The standard deviation of the sample was 0.9 hours. Is it reasonable to conclude that the students at West Virginia sleep less than the typical American? Assume a significance level of .05. (Textbook Problem 10-31)

10-4. According to the Coffee Research Organization (http://www.coffeeresearch.org) the typical American coffee drinker consumes an average of 3.1 cups per day. A sample of 12 senior citizens reveled they consumed the following amounts, reported in cups, of coffee yesterday. (Textbook Problem 10-37)

3.1   3.3   3.5   2.6   2.6   4.3   4.4   3.8   3.1   4.1   3.1   3.2

At the .05 significance level, does this sample data suggest there is a difference between the national average and the sample information from senior citizens?

Chapter 10

10-5. According to the Census Bureau the typical American household includes 3.13 persons. A sample of 25 residents of Arizona retirement communities showed the mean number of residents per household was 2.86. The standard deviation of the sample was 1.20 residents. At the .05 significance level is it reasonable to conclude the mean number of residents in the retirement communities is less than 3.13 persons? (Textbook Problem 10-33)

10-6. A statewide real estate sales agency, Farm Associates, specializes in selling farm property in the state of Nebraska. Their records indicate that the mean selling time of farm property is 90 days. Because of recent drought conditions, they believe that the mean selling time is now greater than 90 days. A statewide survey of 100 farms sold recently revealed that the mean selling time was 94 days, with a standard deviation of 22 days. At the .10 significance level, has there been an increase in selling time?
Textbook Problem (10-32)

10-7. The National Safety Council reported in Vitality that 52 percent of American turnpike drivers are men. A sample of 300 cars traveling eastbound on the New Jersey Turnpike yesterday revealed that 170 were driven by men. At the .01 significance level, can we conclude that a larger proportion of men were driving on the New Jersey Turnpike than the national statistics indicate? (Textbook Problem 10-23)

10-8. The policy of the Suburban Transit Authority is to add a bus route if more than 55 percent of the potential commuters indicate they would use the particular route. A sample of 70 commuters revealed that 42 would use a proposed route from Bowman Park to the downtown area. Does the Bowman-to-downtown route meet the STA criteria? Use the .05 significance level. (Textbook Problem 10 50)

10-9. An urban planner claims that, nationally, 20 percent of all families renting condominiums move during a given year. A random sample of 200 families renting condominiums in the Dallas Metroplex revealed that 56 had moved during the past year. At the .01 significance level, does this evidence suggest that a larger proportion of condominium owners moved in the Dallas area? Determine the p-value. (Textbook Problem 10-53)

CHAPTER
11
TWO-SAMPLE TESTS OF HYPOTHESIS

CHAPTER GOALS

After completing this chapter, you will be able to:

1. Use Excel to conduct a z test of a hypothesis about no difference between two independent population means.

2. Use Excel to conduct a test of hypothesis about no difference between two population proportions.

3. Use Excel to conduct a t test of a hypothesis involving no difference between two population means with unknown standard deviation.

4. Use Excel to conduct a t test of a hypothesis about no mean difference between paired or dependent observations.

Introduction

Chapter 10 dealt with tests of hypothesis using one sample. This chapter will deal with **hypothesis testing of two samples.** As stated in chapter 10, hypothesis testing is a procedure based on sample evidence and probability theory. It is used to determine whether the hypothesis is a reasonable statement and should not be rejected, or is unreasonable and should be rejected.

Steps in hypothesis testing for Two Samples remain the same:

1. **State the null and alternative hypothesis** using either formulas or words. The Null Hypothesis (H_o) is the statement of "no change" or significant difference.

   The Alternative Hypothesis (H_1) is the statement that there is a significant difference. When direction is stated it is a one-directional test (one-tailed). When direction is not stated it is a two-directional test (two-tailed).

2. **Select the level of significance** or the probability that the null hypothesis is rejected when, in fact, it is true.

3. **Select a test statistic** you will be using: the z test, t test, F test, Chi Square test, etc.

4. **Formulate a decision rule.** Using a picture or curve that estimates the distribution you are testing, show the critical value if you are performing a one-directional test or the upper and lower critical values if you are performing a two-directional test.

5. **Make a decision.** State the results of the hypothesis test in terms of the question using complete sentences and examples.

Chapter 11

A Test of Hypothesis Between Sample Means From Two Independent Populations

In the last chapter you created a worksheet used to conduct a test of hypothesis about a sample mean from a single population. You will make some changes to that worksheet to use in other situations. The next will be a test of hypothesis between sample means from two populations. The value of z, the critical value, is computed differently.

$$z = \frac{\overline{X_1} - \overline{X_2}}{\sqrt{\frac{\sigma_1^2}{n_1} + \frac{\sigma_2^2}{n_2}}}$$

$\overline{X_1}$ is the mean of the first sample. It will be referred to as X1_mean.

$\overline{X_2}$ is the mean of the second sample. It will be referred to as X2_mean.

σ_1 is the standard deviation of the first sample (sample1). It will be referred to as s1_StdDev.

σ_2 is the standard deviation of the second sample (sample2). It will be referred to as s2_StdDev.

n_1 is the first sample number. It will be referred to as n1_sample.

n_2 is the second sample number. It will be referred to as n2_sample.

Example 1. Creating a worksheet for testing of hypothesis between two population means.

1. Retrieve the file **1sa-mean**.

2. Make A2 your active cell. Key **Two Sample Means**.

3. Highlight **A5:A8**. From the Home tab, in the Cells group, select the down arrow next to Delete. Select Delete Sheet Rows.

This will delete the contents of the rows and the names of the cells that were created.

4. Highlight **A5:A10**. From the Home tab, in the Cells group, select the down arrow next to Insert. Select Insert Sheet Rows.

This will give you blank rows to insert your input data.

5. In A5:A10, key the input variables, as shown on the next page.

	A	B	C	D	E	F	G	H
1	Test of Normal Hypotheses:							
2	Two Sample Means							
3								
4	Input Data							
5	X1_mean							
6	X2_mean							
7	s1_StdDev							
8	s2_StdDev							
9	n1_sample							
10	n2_sample							
11								

6. Highlight **A5:A10**. From the Home tab, in the Alignment group, select the Align Right icon.

7. Highlight **A5:B10**. From the Formulas tab, in the Defined Names group, select Create from Selection. Select Left Column. Click OK.

8. Make B13 your active cell. You will key a new formula for z. As you key, the formula created for z used with one sample mean will be replaced by the new formula. You will use the shift key with the number 6 to key the ^ symbol. Key **=(X1_mean-X2_mean)/SQRT((s1_StdDev^2/n1_sample)+(s2_StdDev^2/n2_sample))**

z	= =(X1_mean-X2_mean)/SQRT((s1_StdDev^2/n1_sample)+(s2_StdDev^2/

	A	B	
		n2_sample))	
1	Test of Normal Hypotheses:		
2	Two Sample Means		
3			
4	Input Data		
5	X1_mean		
6	X2_mean		
7	s1_StdDev		
8	s2_StdDev		
9	n1_sample		
10	n2_sample		
11	Alpha		
12	Calculated Value		
13	z	#DIV/0!	
14			

Save the worksheet as filename **2sa-mean**.

NOTE: As you work your problems, the answers may differ slightly from the textbook since Excel does not round z and t values. This should not affect the conclusion on whether or not to reject the hypothesis.

Example 2. Tom Sevits is the owner of the Appliance Patch. Recently Tom observed a difference in the dollar value of sales between the men and women he employs as sales associates. A sample of 40 days revealed the men sold a mean of $1,400 worth of appliances per day. For a sample of 50 days, the women sold a mean of $1,500 worth of appliances per day. Assume the population standard deviation for men is $200 and for women $250. At the .05 significance level can Mr. Sevits conclude that the mean amount sold per day is larger for the women? (Since the question is whether or not the mean for women is larger, use women first.)

1. Open the file **2sa-mean** if it is not already active.

2. In B5:B11, enter the input data in the appropriate cells as shown below.

	A	B	C
1	Test of Normal Hypotheses:		
2	Two Sample Means		
3			
4	Input Data		
5	X1_mean	1500	
6	X2_mean	1400	
7	s1_StdDev	250	
8	s2_StdDev	200	
9	n1_sample	50	
10	n2_sample	40	
11	Alpha	0.05	
12			

The values in the output cells have automatically changed to reflect the input data.

B20 f_x =IF(z>RtCrt_zVal, "Reject Ho","Do Not Reject Ho")

	A	B	C	D	E	F	G
1	Test of Normal Hypotheses:						
2	Two Sample Means						
3							
4	Input Data						
5	X1_mean	1500					
6	X2_mean	1400					
7	s1_StdDev	250					
8	s2_StdDev	200					
9	n1_sample	50					
10	n2_sample	40					
11	Alpha	0.05					
12	Calculated Value						
13	z	2.108185					
14	Test for Left-Tail						
15	LftCrt_zVal	-1.64485					
16	Conclusion	Do Not Reject Ho					
17	p-value	0.982493					
18	Test for Right-Tail						
19	RtCrt_zVal	1.644854					
20	Conclusion	Reject Ho					
21	p-value	0.017507					
22	Test for Two-Tail						
23	AbsCrt_zVal	1.959964					
24	Conclusion	Reject Ho					
25	p-value	0.035015					
26							

You can now interpret the results. Since the calculated value for z of 2.108185 is greater than 1.644854, we reject the null hypothesis. This is a one tailed test, and the rejection area is the area greater than 1.644854 (RtCrt_zVal).

The mean amount sold per day is larger for women. The p-value shows that you have a .017507 chance of rejecting a true null hypothesis (a type one error.)

If you wish, save your worksheet as **example2**. Close your file.

A Test of Hypothesis About Two Population Proportions

The last large samples hypothesis with which you will be working is to conduct a test about two population proportions. You will make changes to a previously created worksheet one more time. The formula for finding z changes also.

$$z = \frac{p_1 - p_2}{\sqrt{\frac{p_c(1 - p_c)}{n_1} + \frac{p_c(1 - p_c)}{n_2}}}$$

p_1 is the ratio of the first sample. It will be referred to as p1_ratio.

p_1 is found by the formula $p_1 = \dfrac{X_1}{n_1}$

X_1 is the number in the first sample that possess the trait. It will be referred to as X1_sample.

n_1 is the total number in the first sample. It will be referred to as n1_total.

p_2 is the ratio of the second sample. It will be referred to as p2_ratio.

p_2 is found by the formula $p_2 = \dfrac{X_2}{n_2}$

X_2 is the number in the second sample that possess the trait. It will be referred to as X2_sample.

n_2 is the total number in the second sample. It will be referred to as n2_total.

p_c is the pooled estimate of the population proportion. It will be referred to as pc_est.

p_c is found by the formula $p_c = \dfrac{(X_1 + X_2)}{(n_1 + n_2)}$

Example 3. Creating a worksheet for testing of hypothesis about two population proportions.

1. Retrieve the file **1sa-mean**.

2. Make A2 your active cell. Key **Two Population Proportions**.

3. Highlight **A5:A8**. From the Home tab, in the Cells group, select the down arrow next to Delete. Select Delete Sheet Rows.

This will delete the contents of the rows and the names of the cells that were created.

4. Highlight **A5:A11**. From Home tab, in the Cells group, select the down arrow next to Insert. Select Insert Sheet Rows.

This will give you blank rows to insert your input data.

5. In A5:A11, key the input variable names as shown below.

	A	B	C	D	E	F	G	H
1	Test of Normal Hypotheses:							
2	Two Population Proportions							
3								
4	Input Data							
5	p1_ratio							
6	p2_ratio							
7	X1_sample							
8	X2_sample							
9	n1_total							
10	n2_total							
11	pc_est							
12	Alpha							
13	Calculated Value							
14								

6. Right Align A5:A11.

7. Create names for A5:B11. See page 141 if needed.

8. Make B5 your active cell. Key =**X1_sample/n1_total**

9. Make B6 your active cell. Key **=X2_sample/n2_total**

10. Make B11 your active cell. Key = **(X1_sample+X2_sample)/(n1_total+n2_total)**

11. Make B14 your active cell. As you key, the previous formula for z will be replaced. Key **=(p1_ratio-p2_ratio)/SQRT((pc_est*(1-pc_est)/n1_total)+(pc_est*(1-pc_est)/n2_total))**

	A			
z	▼	=	=(p1_ratio-p2_ratio)/SQRT((pc_est*(1-pc_est)/n1_total)+(pc_est*(1-pc_est)/ n2_total))	
1	Test of Normal Hypotheses:			
2	Two Population Proportions			
3				
4	Input Data			
5	p1_ratio	#DIV/0!		
6	p2_ratio	#DIV/0!		
7	X1_sample			
8	X2_sample			
9	n1_total			
10	n2_total			
11	pc_est	#DIV/0!		
12	Alpha			
13	Calculated Value			
14	z	#DIV/0!		
15				

Save the worksheet as **2-propor**.

Example 4. Of 150 adults who tried a new peach-flavored Peppermint Pattie, 87 rated it excellent. Of 200 children sampled, 123 rated it excellent. Using the .10 level of significance, can we conclude that there is a significant difference in the proportion of adults versus children who rate the new flavor as excellent?

1. Open the file **2-propor** if it is not already active.

2. In B7:B10 and B12, enter the input data in the appropriate cells as shown below.

	A	B	C	D	E	F	G	H
1	Test of Normal Hypotheses:							
2	Two Population Proportions							
3								
4	Input Data							
5	p1_ratio	#DIV/0!						
6	p2_ratio	#DIV/0!						
7	X1_sample	87						
8	X2_sample	123						
9	n1_total	150						
10	n2_total	200						
11	pc_est	#DIV/0!						
12	Alpha	0.1						
13	Calculated Value							
14	z	#VALUE!						
15								

The values in the output cells have automatically changed to reflect the input data.

Chapter 11

	A	B	C	D	E	F	G	H	I
	B25		f_x	=IF(OR(z<-AbsCrt_zVal,z>AbsCrt_zVal), "Reject Ho", "Do Not Reject Ho")					
1	Test of Normal Hypotheses								
2	Two Population Proportions								
3									
4	Input Data								
5	p1_ratio	0.58							
6	p2_ratio	0.615							
7	X1_sample	87							
8	X2_sample	123							
9	n1_total	150							
10	n2_total	200							
11	pc_est	0.6							
12	Alpha	0.1							
13	Calculated Value								
14	z	-0.66144							
15	Test for Left-Tail								
16	LftCrt_zVal	-1.28155							
17	Conclusion	Do Not Reject Ho							
18	p-value	0.254166							
19	Test for Right-Tail								
20	RtCrt_zVal	1.281552							
21	Conclusion	Do Not Reject Ho							
22	p-value	0.745834							
23	Test for Two-Tail								
24	AbsCrt_zVal	1.644854							
25	Conclusion	Do Not Reject Ho							
26	p-value	0.508332							
27									

You can now interpret the results. This is a two-tailed test because there was no direction stated. Accept the null hypothesis. There is not a significant difference in the proportion of adults versus children who rate the candy excellent.

If you wish, save your worksheet as **example4**. Close your file.

Two Population Means with Unknown Standard Deviation

Excel has a pre-prepared dialog box to use for t-tests with two sample means. You will do the following problem using the Data Analysis dialog box:

Example 5. The production manager at Bellevue Steel, a manufacturer of wheelchairs, wants to compare the number of defective wheelchairs produced on the day shift with the number produced on the afternoon shift. A sample of the production from 6 day shifts and 8 afternoon shifts revealed the following number of defects:

Day	5	8	7	6	9	7		
Afternoon	8	10	7	11	9	12	14	9

At the .05 significance level, is there a difference in the mean number of defects per shift?

1. In a new worksheet, in cells A1:B9, key the data for Day and Afternoon as shown below.

	A	B	C	D	E	F	G	H	I	
1	Day	Afternoon								
2	5	8								
3	8	10								
4	7	7								
5	6	11								
6	9	9								
7	7	12								
8		14								
9		9								
10										

Make sure you have a **Data Analysis** command in your **Data** tab. If **Data Analysis** does not appear, select **Add-Ins**. See Page 43, instructions 2–4.

2. From the **Data** tab, in the **Analysis** group select **Data Analysis**. Place your mouse arrow on the down arrow of the side scroll bar. Select **t-Test: Two Sample Assuming Equal Variances**. Click **OK**.

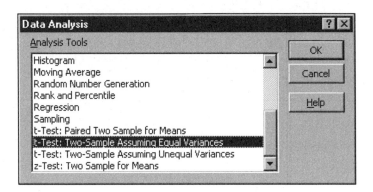

The dialog box for t-Test: Two Sample Assuming Equal Variances is displayed.

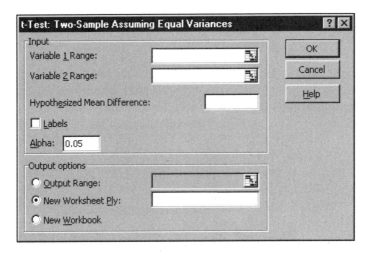

3. Your cursor should be on the Variable 1 Range text box: Key **A1:A7**. Touch the tab key.

4. In the Variable 2 Range: text box, key **B1:B9**. Touch the tab key.

5. In the Hypothesized Mean Difference text box, key **0**. Touch the tab key.

6. Select the Labels check box. Touch the tab key.

7. In the Alpha text box, key **.05** if it is not already displayed.

8. Select the Output Range check box. In the text box, key **E1**. Click OK.

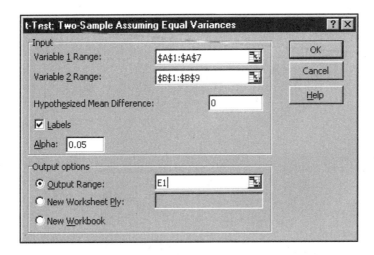

The output data is displayed, but is hard to read.

	A	B	C	D	E	F	G	H	I
1	Day	Afternoon			t-Test: Two-Sample Assuming Equal Variances				
2	5	8							
3	8	10				Day	Afternoon		
4	7	7			Mean	7	10		
5	6	11			Variance	2	5.142857		
6	9	9			Observati	6	8		
7	7	12			Pooled Va	3.833333			
8		14			Hypothesi	0			
9		9			df	12			
10					t Stat	-2.8372			
11					P(T<=t) on	0.007487			
12					t Critical o	1.782288			
13					P(T<=t) tw	0.014974			
14					t Critical t	2.178813			
15									

Make E8 your active cell. From the **Home** tab, in the **Cells** group, select the **down arrow** next to **Format**. Under **Cell Size**, select **AutoFit Column Width**.

	A	B	C	D	E	F	G	H
1	Day	Afternoon			t-Test: Two-Sample Assuming Equal Variances			
2	5	8						
3	8	10				Day	Afternoon	
4	7	7			Mean	7	10	
5	6	11			Variance	2	5.142857	
6	9	9			Observations	6	8	
7	7	12			Pooled Variance	3.833333		
8		14			Hypothesized Mean Difference	0		
9		9			df	12		
10					t Stat	-2.8372		
11					P(T<=t) one-tail	0.007487		
12					t Critical one-tail	1.782288		
13					P(T<=t) two-tail	0.014974		
14					t Critical two-tail	2.178813		
15								

The output is now easier to read and can be interpreted.

Reject the H_o and accept the H_1. The computed t statistic (–2.8372) is less than the negative critical value for a two tailed t test (–2.178813).* There is a difference in the mean number of defects between the afternoon shift and the day shift at the .05 level of significance. (* H_o is rejected if the t Stat is greater than the t Critical two-tail or less than a negative value of the t Critical two-tail.)

Save as **ex5t-tst**.

Chapter 11

Paired or Dependent Observations

Excel also has a dialog box to use with paired observations. You will do the following problem using the Data Analysis dialog box.

Example 6. Advertisements by Sylph Fitness Center claim that completion of their course will result in the loss of weight. A random sample of 8 recent students showed the following body weights before entering the course and after the completion of the course. At the .01 significance level can we conclude that the students lost weight?

Name	Before	After
Hunter	155	154
Cashman	228	207
Mervine	141	147
Massa	162	157
Cerola	211	196
Peterson	164	150
Redding	184	170
Poust	172	165

1. Open the file **ex5t-tst**. On this same worksheet, beginning with row 16, enter the data in columns A, B, and C as shown below.

	A	B	C	D	E	F	G	H
1	Day	Afternoon			t-Test: Two-Sample Assuming Equal Variances			
2	5	8						
3	8	10				Day	Afternoon	
4	7	7			Mean	7	10	
5	6	11			Variance	2	5.142857	
6	9	9			Observations	6	8	
7	7	12			Pooled Variance	3.833333		
8		14			Hypothesized Mean Difference	0		
9		9			df	12		
10					t Stat	-2.8372		
11					P(T<=t) one-tail	0.007487		
12					t Critical one-tail	1.782288		
13					P(T<=t) two-tail	0.014974		
14					t Critical two-tail	2.178813		
15								
16	Name	Before	After					
17	Hunter	155	154					
18	Cashman	228	207					
19	Mervine	141	147					
20	Massa	162	157					
21	Cerola	211	196					
22	Peterson	164	150					
23	Redding	184	170					
24	Poust	172	165					
25								

Make sure you have a **Data Analysis** command in your **Data** tab. If **Data Analysis** does not appear, select **A̲dd-Ins**. See Page 43, instructions 2–4.

2. From the **Data** tab, in the **Analysis** group select **Data Analysis**. Place your mouse arrow on the down arrow of the side scroll bar. Select **t-Test: Paired Two Samples for Means**. Click **OK**.

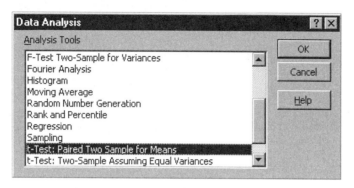

The dialog box for t-Test: Paired Two Sample for Means, is displayed.

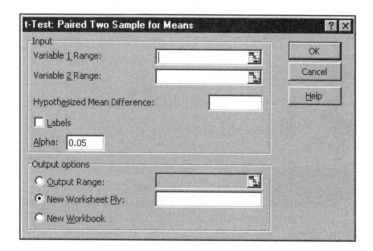

3. Your cursor should be in the **Variable 1̲ Range** text box. Key **B16:B24**. Touch the tab key.

4. In the **Variable 2̲ Range** text box, key **C16:C24**. Touch the tab key.

5. In the **Hypoth̲esized Mean Difference** text box, key **0**. Touch the tab key.

6. Select the **Labels** check box. Touch the tab key.

7. In the **Alpha** text box, key **.01**.

8. Select the Output Range check box. In the text box, key **E16**. Click OK.

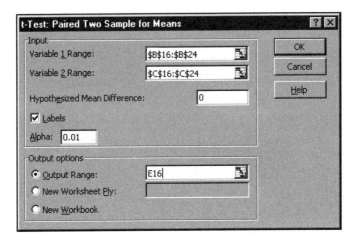

The output data is displayed.

	A	B	C	D	E	F	G	H
16	Name	Before	After		t-Test: Paired Two Sample for Means			
17	Hunter	155	154					
18	Cashman	228	207			Before	After	
19	Mervine	141	147		Mean	177.125	168.25	
20	Massa	162	157		Variance	857.8393	485.6429	
21	Cerola	211	196		Observations	8	8	
22	Peterson	164	150		Pearson Correlation	0.981101		
23	Redding	184	170		Hypothesized Mean Difference	0		
24	Poust	172	165		df	7		
25					t Stat	2.861003		
26					P(T<=t) one-tail	0.012151		
27					t Critical one-tail	2.997952		
28					P(T<=t) two-tail	0.024303		
29					t Critical two-tail	3.499483		
30								

Accept the H₀. The computed t statistic (2.861003) is less than the t Critical one-tail (2.997952). We cannot conclude that the students lost weight at the .01 level of significance.

Chapter 11

You can use worksheets for more than one problem. Since these are both t-tests we put them on the same worksheet. Make sure you use the same column for the output so the labels are in the same expanded column.

If you wish, you may print both exercises 5 and 6.

	A	B	C	D	E	F	G	H
1	Day	Afternoon			t-Test: Two-Sample Assuming Equal Variances			
2	5	8						
3	8	10				Day	Afternoon	
4	7	7			Mean	7	10	
5	6	11			Variance	2	5.142857	
6	9	9			Observations	6	8	
7	7	12			Pooled Variance	3.833333		
8		14			Hypothesized Mean Difference	0		
9		9			df	12		
10					t Stat	-2.8372		
11					P(T<=t) one-tail	0.007487		
12					t Critical one-tail	1.782288		
13					P(T<=t) two-tail	0.014974		
14					t Critical two-tail	2.178813		
15								
16	Name	Before	After		t-Test: Paired Two Sample for Means			
17	Hunter	155	154					
18	Cashman	228	207			Before	After	
19	Mervine	141	147		Mean	177.125	168.25	
20	Massa	162	157		Variance	857.8393	485.6429	
21	Cerola	211	196		Observations	8	8	
22	Peterson	164	150		Pearson Correlation	0.981101		
23	Redding	184	170		Hypothesized Mean Difference	0		
24	Poust	172	165		df	7		
25					t Stat	2.861003		
26					P(T<=t) one-tail	0.012151		
27					t Critical one-tail	2.997952		
28					P(T<=t) two-tail	0.024303		
29					t Critical two-tail	3.499483		
30								

If you wish, save as **ex5&6t-tst**. Close your file.

149

Practice Exercises taken from textbook.

In addition to showing your printout, state the results of the hypothesis test in terms of the question using complete sentences and examples.

11-1. A nationwide sample of influential Republicans and Democrats were asked as a part of a comprehensive survey whether they favored lowering the environmental standards so that high-sulfur coal could be burned in coal-fired power plants. The results were: (Textbook Problem 11-11)

	Republicans	Democrats
Number sampled	1,000	800
Number in favor	200	168

At the .02 level of significance, can we conclude that there is a larger proportion of Democrats in favor of lowering the standards?

11-2. Fry Brothers heating and Air Conditioning, Inc. employs Larry Clark and George Murnen to make service calls to repair furnaces and air conditioning units in homes. Tom Fry, the owner, would like to know whether there is a difference in the mean number of service calls they make per day. Assume the population standard deviation for Larry Clark is 1.05 calls per day and 1.23 calls per day for George Murnen. A random sample of 40 days last year showed that Larry Clark made an average of 4.77 calls per day. For a sample of 50 days George Murnen made an average of 5.02 calls per day. At the .05 significance level, is there a difference in the mean number of calls per day between the two employees. What is the p-value? (Textbook Problem 11-25)

11-3. A study was conducted to determine if there was a difference in the humor content in British and American trade magazine advertisements. In an independent random sample of 270 American trade magazine advertisements. 56 were humorous. An independent random sample of 203 British trade magazines contained 52 humorous ads. Does this data provide evidence at the .05 significance level that there is a difference in the proportion of humorous ads in British versus American trade magazines? (Textbook Problem 11-34)

11-4. As part of a recent survey among dual-wage-earner couples, an industrial psychologist found that 990 men out of the 1,500 surveyed believed that division of household duties was fair. A sample of 1,600 women found that 970 believed the division of household duties was fair. At the .01 significance level, is it reasonable to conclude that the proportion of men who believe the division of household duties is fair is larger? (Textbook Problem 11-31)

11-5. The federal government recently granted funds for a special program designed to reduce crime in high-crime areas. A study of the results of the program in eight high-crime areas of Miami, FL, yielded the following results. (Textbook Problem 11-22)

Number of Crimes by Area

	A	B	C	D	E	F	G	H
Before	14	7	4	5	17	12	8	9
After	2	7	3	6	8	13	3	5

Has there been a decrease in the number of crimes since the inauguration of the program? Use the .01 significance level.

11-6. Each month the National Association of Purchasing Managers publishes the NAPM index. One of the questions asked on the survey to purchasing agents is: Do you think the economy is contracting? Last month of the 300 responses, 160 answered the yes to the question. This month 170 of the 290 responses indicated they felt the economy was contracting. At the .05 significance level can we conclude that a larger proportion of the agents believe the economy is contracting this month? (Textbook Problem 11-30)

11-7. A number of minor automobile accidents occur at various high-risk intersections in Teton County despite traffic lights. The traffic department claims that a modification in the type of light will reduce these accidents. The county commissioners have agreed to a proposed experiment. Eight intersections were chosen at random, and the lights at those intersections were modified. The numbers of minor accidents during a six-month period before and after the modifications were: (Textbook Problem 11-38)

Number of accidents, by intersection

	A	B	C	D	E	F	G	H
Before modification	5	7	6	4	8	9	8	10
After modification	3	7	7	0	4	6	8	2

At the .01 significance level is it reasonable to conclude that the modification reduced the number of traffic accidents?

CHAPTER
12
ANALYSIS OF VARIANCE

CHAPTER GOALS

After completing this chapter, you will be able to:

1. List the characteristics of the F distribution.

2. Discuss the general idea of analysis of variance.

3. Use Excel to conduct a hypothesis test to determine if two sample variances came from similar populations.

4. Use Excel to set up and organize data into an ANOVA table.

Introduction

In this chapter we will continue to discuss hypothesis testing by introducing the F distribution. The F distribution is used as the test statistic for several situations. It is used to test whether two samples are from populations having equal variances, and it is also applied when we want to compare more than two population means simultaneously. The simultaneous comparison of several population means is called **analysis of variance (ANOVA).** In both of these situations, the populations must be normal, and the data must be at least interval-scale.

Characteristics of the F Distribution

- There is a "family" of F distributions. A particular member of the family is determined by two parameters: the degrees of freedom in the numerator and the degrees of freedom in the denominator.

- F cannot be negative, and it is a continuous distribution.

- The curve representing an F distribution is positively skewed.

- It is asymptotic. Its values range from 0 to infinity. As the values of F increases, the curve approaches the X-axis, but it never touches it.

Steps in hypothesis testing:

1. **State the null and alternative hypothesis** using either formulas or words.
   The Null Hypothesis (H_o)   is always the statement of no significant difference.

   The Alternative Hypothesis (H_1) is always the statement that there is a significant difference. When direction is stated it is a one-directional test (one-tailed). When direction is not stated it is a two-directional test (two-tailed).

2. **State the level of significance** or the probability that the null hypothesis is rejected when, in fact, it is true.

3. **State the statistical test** you will be using: the z test, t test, F test, Chi Square test, etc.

4. **Formulate a decision rule**. Using a picture or curve that estimates the distribution you are testing, show the critical value if you are performing a one-directional test or the upper and lower critical values if you are performing a two-directional test.

5. **Do it**. Show the formula you used and at least the major steps involved. State the results of the hypothesis test in terms of the question using complete sentences and examples.

F-Test Two-Sample for Variances

Excel has a data analysis program for finding an F-test for two sample variances.

Example 1. Lammers Limos offers limousine service from the city hall in Toledo, Ohio to Metro Airport in Detroit. Sean Lammers, president of the company, is considering two routes. One is via U.S. 25 and the other via I-75. He wants to study the time it takes to drive to the airport using each route and then compare the results. He collected the following sample data, which is reported in minutes. Using the .10 significance level, is there a difference in the variation in the driving times for the two routes?

Route 25	52	67	56	45	70	54	64	
InSt 75	59	60	61	51	56	63	57	65

Since this is a two tailed test the significance level used is .05.

1. In a new worksheet, key the data as shown.

	A	B	C
1	Route 25	InSt 75	
2	52	59	
3	67	60	
4	56	61	
5	45	51	
6	70	56	
7	54	63	
8	64	57	
9		65	
10			

Make sure you have a **Data Analysis** command in your **Data** tab. If **Data Analysis** does not appear, select <u>A</u>dd-Ins. See Page 43, instructions 2 – 4.

    2.   From the **Data** tab, in the **Analysis** group select **Data Analysis**. Select **F-Test Two Sample for Variances**. Click **OK**.

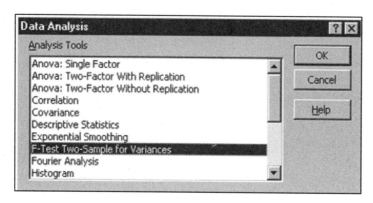

The dialog box for F-Test Two-Sample for Variances, is displayed.

    3.   Your cursor should be on the Variable <u>1</u> Range text box. Key **A1:A8**. Touch the **tab** key.

    4.   In the Variable 2 Range text box, key **B1:B9**. Touch the **tab** key.

    5.   Select <u>L</u>abels, check box. Touch the **tab** key.

    6.   The <u>A</u>lpha text box should have **.05**.

    7.   Select <u>O</u>utput Range, check box. In the <u>O</u>utput Range text box, key **D1**. Click **OK**.

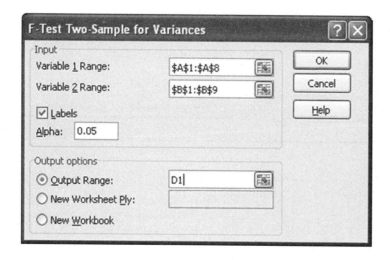

Chapter 12

The output box is displayed but is difficult to read.

	A	B	C	D	E	F	G
1	Route 25	InSt 75		F-Test Two-Sample for Variances			
2	52	59					
3	67	60			Route 25	InSt 75	
4	56	61		Mean	58.28571	59	
5	45	51		Variance	80.90476	19.14286	
6	70	56		Observati	7	8	
7	54	63		df	6	7	
8	64	57		F	4.226368		
9		65		P(F<=f) on	0.040397		
10				F Critical c	3.865969		
11							

8. Make D10 your active cell. From the Home tab, in the Cells group, select the down arrow next to Format. Under Cell Size, select AutoFit Column Width.

	A	B	C	D	E	F
1	Route 25	InSt 75		F-Test Two-Sample for Variances		
2	52	59				
3	67	60			Route 25	InSt 75
4	56	61		Mean	58.28571	59
5	45	51		Variance	80.90476	19.14286
6	70	56		Observations	7	8
7	54	63		df	6	7
8	64	57		F	4.226368	
9		65		P(F<=f) one-tail	0.040397	
10				F Critical one-tail	3.865969	
11						

Your table in now easier to read and can be interpreted.

The null hypothesis is rejected because the computed value for F 4.226368 is greater than the critical value of 3.865969. There is a difference in the variance of the travel times along the two routes.

If you wish, save your file as **ex1-var**. Close your file.

NOTE: As you work your problems, the answers may differ slightly from the textbook since Excel does not round F values. This should <u>not</u> affect the conclusion on whether or not to reject the hypothesis.

156

Single Factor Analysis of Variance

Excel has a data analysis program for finding analysis of variance (ANOVA).

Example 2. Citrus Cleaner is a new all-purpose cleaner being test marketed by placing displays in three different locations within various supermarkets. The number of 12-ounce bottles sold from each location within the supermarket is reported below.

Near bread	Near beer	Other cleaners
18	12	26
14	18	28
19	10	30
17	16	32

At the .05 significance level, is there a difference in the mean number of bottles sold at the three locations?

1. In a new worksheet, key the data as shown below.

	A	B	C	D
1	Near bread	Near beer	Other cleaners	
2	18	12	26	
3	14	18	28	
4	19	10	30	
5	17	16	32	
6				

Make sure you have a **Data Analysis** command in your **Data** tab. If **Data Analysis** does not appear, select **Add-Ins**. See Page 43, instructions 2 – 4.

2. From the **Data** tab, in the **Analysis** group select **Data Analysis**. Select **Anova: Single Factor**. Click **OK**.

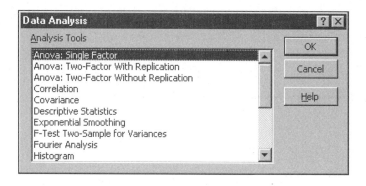

The dialog box for Anova: Single Factor, is displayed.

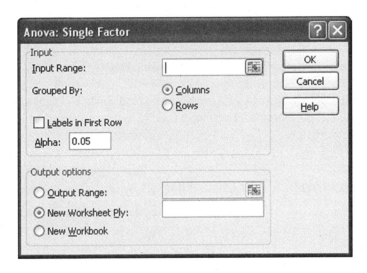

3. Your cursor should be on the Input Range text box. Key **A1:C5**. Touch the **tab** key.

4. **Grouped by Columns** should be selected. Touch the **tab** key.

5. Select Labels in First Row, check box. Touch the **tab** key.

6. The Alpha text box should have .05.

7. Select Output Range, check box. In the Output Range text box, key **A8**. Click **OK**.

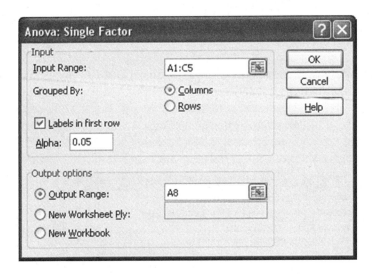

The output box is now displayed but it is difficult to read.

	A	B	C	D	E	F	G	H
1	Near brea	Near beer	Other cleaners					
2	18	12	26					
3	14	18	28					
4	19	10	30					
5	17	16	32					
6								
7								
8	Anova: Single Factor							
9								
10	SUMMARY							
11	Groups	Count	Sum	Average	Variance			
12	Near brea	4	68	17	4.666667			
13	Near beer	4	56	14	13.33333			
14	Other clea	4	116	29	6.666667			
15								
16								
17	ANOVA							
18	ce of Varic	SS	df	MS	F	P-value	F crit	
19	Between (	504	2	252	30.64865	9.61E-05	4.256495	
20	Within Gr	74	9	8.222222				
21								
22	Total	578	11					
23								

8. Make A18 your active cell. From the **Home** tab, in the **Cells** group, select the **down arrow** next to **Format**. Under **Cell Size**, select **AutoFit Column Width**.

	A	B	C	D	E	F	G	H
1	Near bread		Near beer	Other cleaners				
2		18	12	26				
3		14	18	28				
4		19	10	30				
5		17	16	32				
6								
7								
8	Anova: Single Factor							
9								
10	SUMMARY							
11	Groups	Count	Sum	Average	Variance			
12	Near bread	4	68	17	4.666667			
13	Near beer	4	56	14	13.33333			
14	Other cleaners	4	116	29	6.666667			
15								
16								
17	ANOVA							
18	Source of Variation	SS	df	MS	F	P-value	F crit	
19	Between Groups	504	2	252	30.64865	9.61E-05	4.256495	
20	Within Groups	74	9	8.222222				
21								
22	Total	578	11					
23								

Your table is now easier to read and can be interpreted.

The computed F of 30.64865 is greater than the F critical value of 4.256495 so we reject the null hypothesis. There is a difference in the mean number of bottles sold at the various locations.

If you wish, save your file as **ex2-var**. Close your file.

Practice Exercises taken from textbook.

In addition to showing your printout, state the results of the hypothesis test in terms of the question using complete sentences and examples.

12-1. There are two Chevrolet Dealers in Jamestown, NY. The mean weekly sales at Sharkey Chevy and Dave White Chevrolet are about the same. However, Tom Sharkey, the owner of Sharkey Chevy, believes his sales are more consistent. Below is the number of new cars sold at Sharkey in the last seven months, and for the last eight months at Dave White. Do you agree with Mr. Sharkey? Use the .01 significance level. (Textbook Problem 12-17) Hint: Use variable 1 as Dave White and variable 2 as Sharkey.

Dave White				Sharkey			
75	81	81	30	98	78	54	57
82	46	58	101	68	64	70	

12-2. A consumer organization wants to know if there is a difference in the price of a particular toy at three different types of stores. The price of the toy was checked in a sample of five discount toy stores, five variety stores, and five department stores. The results are shown below. Use the .05 significance level. (Textbook Problem 12-21)

Discount toy	Variety	Department
$12	$15	$19
13	17	17
14	14	16
12	18	20
15	17	19

12-3. Suppose that 14 randomly selected students were divided into two groups, one consisting of 6 students and the other of 8. One group was taught using a combination of lecture and programmed instruction, the other using a combination of lecture and television. At the end of the course, each group was given a 50-item test. The following is a list of the number correct for each of the two groups. (Textbook Problem 12-25)

Lecture and Programmed Instruction	Lecture and Television
19	32
17	28
23	31
22	26
17	23
16	24
	27
	25

Using the analysis of variance technique, test H_o that the two test scores are equal. Use a significance level of .05.

12-4. Jacob Lee is a frequent traveler between Los Angles and San Francisco. For the past month, he wrote down the flight times on three different airlines. The results are : (Textbook Problem 12-22)

Goust	Jet Red	Cloudtran
51	50	52
51	53	55
52	52	60
42	62	64
51	53	61
57	49	49
47	50	49
47	49	
50	58	
60	54	
54	51	
49	49	
48	49	
48	50	

Use the .05 significance level and the five-step hypothesis-testing process to check if there is a difference in the mean flight times among the three airlines.

12-5. The city of Maumee comprises four districts. Chief of Police Andy North wants to determine whether there is a difference in the mean number of crimes committed among the four districts. He recorded the number of crimes reported in each district for a sample of six days. At the .05 significance level, can the chief of police conclude there is a difference in the mean number of crimes? (Textbook Problem 12-23)

	Number of Crimes		
Rec Center	Key Street	Monclova	Whitehouse
13	21	12	16
15	13	14	17
14	18	15	18
15	19	13	15
14	18	12	20
15	19	15	18

CHAPTER
13
LINEAR REGRESSION AND CORRELATION

CHAPTER GOALS

After completing this chapter, you will be able to:

1. Explain correlation and regression.

2. Use Excel to draw a scatter diagram.

3. Use Excel to calculate the coefficient of determination.

4. Use Excel to find a least squares regression line.

5. Use Excel and the least squares regression equation to predict the value of a dependent variable based on an independent variable.

Introduction

The emphasis in this chapter is studying the relationship between two numbers and developing an equation that allows us to estimate one variable based on another. Is there a relationship between the temperature and the number of people on the beach? Is there a relationship between education and monthly earnings? Can we predict our grade on the next statistics test based on how much time we spend studying the material on the test?

Correlation analysis is a group of statistical techniques used to measure the strength of the relationship (correlation) between two variables. The **dependent variable**, the variable being predicted or estimated is shown on the vertical axis (Y-axis) and the **independent variable**, the predictor variable which provides the basis for estimation is shown on the horizontal axis (X-axis). The **coefficient of correlation** may assume any value on a scale of -1 to +1, inclusive. It describes the strength of the relationship between two sets of interval-scaled or ratio-scaled variables. A correlation coefficient of -1 or +1 indicates a perfect correlation. A coefficient of correlation close to 0 shows a weak relationship.

Terms such as weak, moderate, and strong, however, do not have precise meaning. A measure that has a more exact meaning is the **coefficient of determination**. It is computed by squaring the coefficient of correlation. The coefficient of determination is the total variation in the dependent variable Y that is explained, or accounted, for by the variation in the independent variable X.

Regression analysis is a technique used to express the relationship between two variables that estimates the value of the dependent variable Y based on a selected value of the independent variable X. The **least squares regression equation** ($\hat{Y} = a + bX$) is the mathematical equation that defines the relationship between two variables that have a linear relationship.

a   is the estimated value of the dependent variable Y where the regression line crosses the Y-axis when X is zero.

b   is the slope of the line, or the average change in $\hat{Y}$ for each change of one unit (either increase or decrease) in the independent variable X.

The following examples show how you can use Excel to work with correlation and regression analysis:

Like chapter 4 we will use Excel to plot a scatter diagram. In this chapter we will add a least squares regression line which will be used to help determine a coefficient of determination. Then we will develop a regression equation to use in predicting a dependent value, given the independent value.

Scatter Diagrams and Least Squares Regression Line

Example 1. Haverty's Furniture is a family business that has been selling to retail customers in the Chicago area for many years. They advertise extensively on radio, TV and the internet emphasizing their low prices and easy credit terms. The owner would like to review the relationship between sales (in millions of dollars) and the amount spent on advertising (in millions of dollars). Below is information on sales and advertising expense for the last four months.

Month	Advertising expense ($million)	Sales revenue ($million)
July	2	7
August	1	3
September	3	8
October	4	10

The owner wants to forecast sales based on advertising expense.

a.   Draw a scatter diagram with a least squares regression line.

b.   What is the coefficient of determination?

c.   Assuming a normal distribution, using the regression equation, (1) estimate the revenue for an advertising expense of 1.5 million dollars, (2) estimate the revenue for an advertising expense of 3.5 million dollars.

Creating a scatter diagram with a least squares regression line.

NOTE: When entering the data you <u>must</u> put the data for the independent variable **first**.

1.   On a new worksheet, enter the data for the problem as shown. Notice that the data for Advertising is entered first since it is the independent variable.

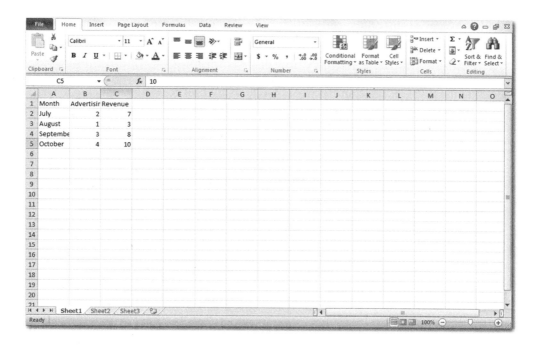

2. Highlight **B2:C5**. From the Insert tab, in the Charts group select Scatter.

3. Select the 1st upper left chart, Scatter with only Markers.

4. From the Design tab in the Chart Layouts group, select Layout 1.

5. In your chart, click on the Chart Title. A box appears around it. Key **Correlation Between Advertising and Revenue.** As you type the title shows in the equation box. Push <Enter>. The title is displayed in the chart. In the chart, click on the Horizontal (Category) Axis Title. Key **Advertising**. Push <Enter>. In the chart, click on the Vertical (Value) Axis Title. Key **Revenue**. Push <Enter>.

6. Place your cursor on Series 1 Legend Entry. Click your right mouse button. Select Delete.

The scatter chart is formed.

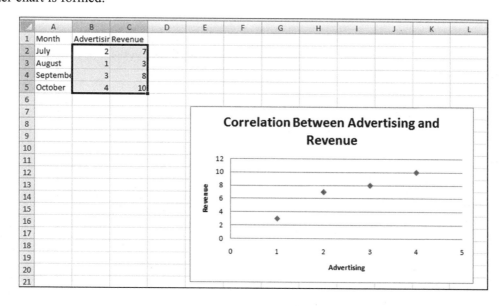

7. With the handles still on the chart, click and hold the left mouse button inside the chart. A 4-way arrow will show in the chart. As you move the chart it will show as an open box. Move the chart so the upper left corner is in cell D1 and move the right border to the middle of column I so it will fit on one page.

8. Point to the title **Correlation Between Advertising and Revenue**. Click your right mouse. Two dialog boxes appear. Click your mouse on the font size down arrow. Choose **14**.

The chart will on fit on one page.

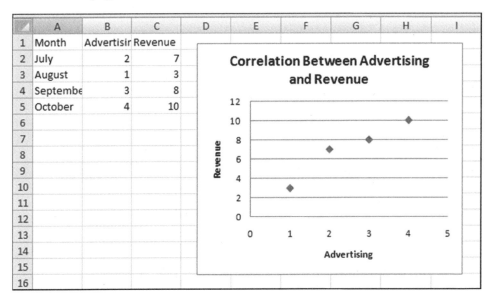

You will now add a least squares regression line or a *trendline*.

9. Make sure the handles show on the chart box. With your mouse, right click on one of the data points. There will be a box around each data point.

10. From the pull down list, select Add Trendline.

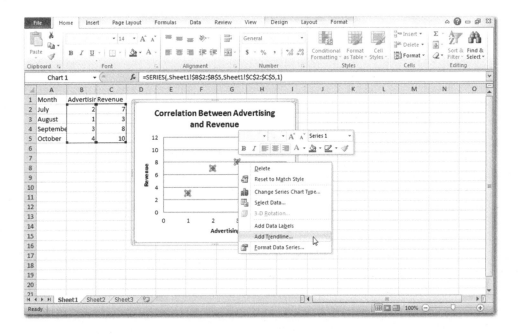

The Format Trendline dialog box appears.

11. Under **Trendline Options, Linear** should be selected for **Trend/Regression type**.

12. **Automatic** should be selected under **Trendline name**. Select the check boxes for **Display Equation on chart** and **Display R-squared value on chart**. Click **Close**.

The regression equation and R^2 are shown, but hard to read.

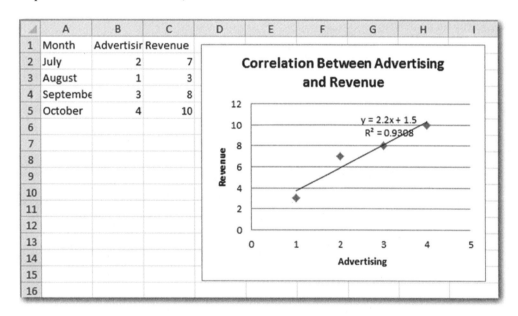

13. Click anywhere on the equation. A box appears around the outside. Click, hold and drag the box next to the word Revenue.

The equation $y = 2.2x + 1.5$ and $R^2 = 0.9308$ is now off the chart and is easier to read.

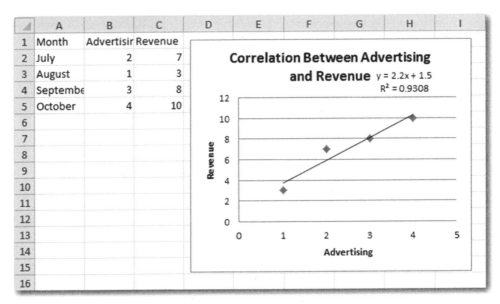

Example 2. Since you requested Excel to display the R^2 value on the chart, you can read from the chart that the coefficient of determination is .9308.

On the same worksheet containing your chart, in A7, key **Coeffic of determ = .9308**.

Example 3. You will use the regression equation to estimate the revenue based on the amount spent on advertising (x). The equation is $\hat{Y} = a + bX$, or y = bx + a as used in Excel.

Since you requested Excel to display the equation on the chart, you can use the given equation for your estimate. The equation on the chart uses "y" instead of "$\hat{Y}$" and has "a" and "bx" in reverse order, but otherwise it is the same equation. 1.5 is the value of "a" and 2.2 is the value of "b".

1. On the same worksheet containing your chart, in cells A9:B12, enter the information as shown.

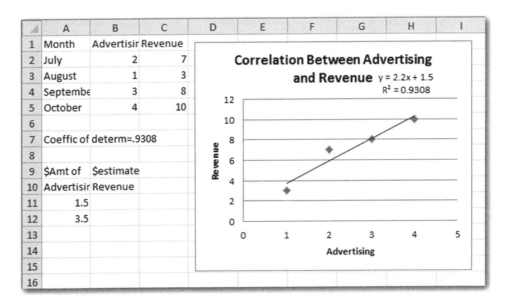

2. In B11, key =**1.5+2.2*A11**

3. Copy B11 to B12.

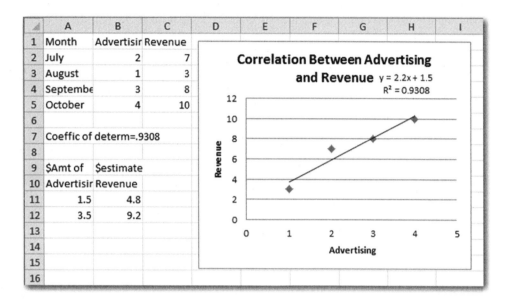

This computes the estimated revenue for both amounts of advertising and completes your problem.

If you wish, save your file as **linreg-1**. Close your file.

Practice Exercises taken from textbook.

13-1. The Bardi Trucking Co., located in Cleveland, Ohio, makes deliveries in the Great Lakes region, the Southeast, and the Northeast. Jim Bardi, the president, is studying the relationship between the distance a shipment must travel and the length of time, in days, it takes the shipment to arrive at its destination. To investigate, Mr. Bardi selected a random sample of 20 shipments made last month. Shipping distance is the independent variable, and shipping time is the dependent variable. The results are as follows. (Textbook Problem 13-51)

Shipment	Distance (miles)	Shipping time (days)
1	656	5
2	853	14
3	646	6
4	783	11
5	610	8
6	841	10
7	785	9
8	639	9
9	762	10
10	762	9
11	862	7
12	679	5
13	835	13
14	607	3
15	665	8
16	647	7
17	685	10
18	720	8
19	652	6
20	828	10

a. Draw a scatter diagram, add Trendline, display equation and R-squared value on chart.
b. Determine and interpret the coefficient of determination.
c. What would be the estimated shipping time for a distance of 715 miles?

13-2. The manufacturer of Cardio Glide exercise equipment wants to study the relationship between the number of months since the glide was purchased and the length of time the equipment was used last week. (Textbook Problem 13-45)

Person	Months owned	Hours exercised	Person	Months owned	Hours exercised
Rupple	12	4	Massa	2	8
Hall	2	10	Sass	8	3
Bennett	6	8	Karl	4	8
Longnecker	9	5	Malrooney	10	2
Phillips	7	5	Veights	5	5

a. Plot the information on a scatter diagram. Let the hours of exercise be the dependent variable. Add a Trendline. Display equation and R-squared value on chart.
b. Determine and interpret the coefficient of determination.
c. What would be the estimated number of hours exercised on a glide owned 11 months?

CHAPTER
14
MULTIPLE REGRESSION AND CORRELATION ANALYSIS

CHAPTER GOALS

After completing this chapter, you will be able to:

1. Explain multiple regression and correlation.

2. Use Excel to calculate the multiple coefficient of determination.

3. Use Excel to describe the relationship between two or more independent variables and a dependent variable using a multiple regression equation.

4. Use Excel and the least squares regression equation to predict the value of a dependent variable based on two or more independent variables.

Introduction

Chapter 13 explained regression and correlation analysis, which allowed us to estimate one variable based on another. The use of only one independent variable to predict the dependent variable ignores the relationship of other variables to the dependent variable. This chapter expands the concept by allowing us to use more than one explanatory variable in a regression equation. Using more than one independent variable makes it possible to increase the explanatory power and the usefulness of regression and correlation analysis in making many business decisions.

This chapter shows you how to use Excel to find a multiple regression equation, predict a dependent variable based on two or more independent variables and find the multiple coefficient of determination.

The following example will show how you can use Excel to work with multiple regression and correlation.

Multiple Regression and Correlation.

The multiple regression model allows one to predict the value of a dependent variable by incorporating two or more independent variables.

The textbook states the estimated multiple regression model as $\hat{Y} = a + b_1X_1 + b_2X_2 + \ldots b_kX_k$. Excel uses the "least squares" method to calculate a straight line that best fits the data and returns an array that describes the line. The multiple regression equation for the line is: $y = m_1x_1 + m_2x_2 + \ldots m_nx_n + b$.

You will use the LINEST function of Excel. LINEST gives you the means to predict the dependent variable and the coefficient of determination.

The LINEST function is written, **=LINEST(known_y's,known_x's,const,stats)** , where:

known_y's is the range of y-values you already know

known_x's is the range of the known variables

const is a logical whether or not to calculate the constant normally. For these problems it will always be TRUE.

stats is a logical value specifying whether to return additional regression statistics such as the coefficient of determination. Since you want the additional statistics, it will always be TRUE.

The *array* that LINEST *returns* is $\{m_n, m_{n-1},...m_1, b\}$. So the coefficients that correspond to each x-value in the array are the **reverse** of the coefficients in the multiple regression equation for the line. When entering the data into Excel, you must enter the data for the independent variables **first**, then your known Y values.

Example. The quality control engineer at steel company is interested in estimating the tensile strength of steel wire based on its outside diameter and the amount of molybdenum in the steel. As an experiment, she selected four pieces of wire, measured the outside diameters, and determined the molybdenum content. Then she measured the tensile strength of each piece. The results were:

Piece	Tensile Strength (psi) Y	Outside diameter (cm) X1	Amount of molybdenum (units) X2
A	11	3	6
B	9	2	5
C	16	4	8
D	12	3	7

Using a multiple regression equation, what is the estimated tensile strength of a steel wire having an outside diameter of 3.5 cm and 6.4 units of molybdenum? What is the multiple coefficient of determination?

You will use the LINEST function to calculate coefficients needed in the multiple regression to predict the tensile strength of the steel wire. Notice the independent variables of X2 and X1 were entered first, then the known Y values. In the multiple regression line, Excel reverses the order of the coefficients from the way they were listed in the worksheet. If you enter the independent variables in reverse order they will be correct in the multiple regression equation.

1. On a new worksheet, enter the data as shown.

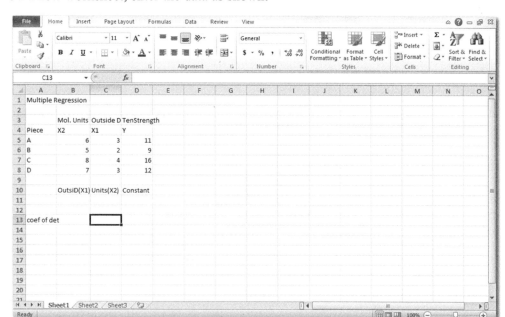

Notice that where the answers will be displayed, you place the coefficients in reverse order of the way they were entered on the worksheet. The LINEST function always displays the constant value last. **Be sure** when you key the LINEST function you list the cell contents for the known **Y values first**.

2. Highlight **B11:D13**. With the range still highlighted, key
   =LINEST(D5:D8,B5:C8,TRUE,TRUE) <u>DO NOT TOUCH THE <ENTER> KEY YET!</u>

3. After you have finished keying, hold down the **<Shift>** key and the **<Ctrl>** key together and at the same time touch the **<Enter>** key. The formula in the formula bar at the top of the worksheet should be inside curly brackets, {}.

	A	B	C	D	E	F	G	H	I
1	Multiple Regression								
2									
3		Mol. Units	Outside D	TenStrength					
4	Piece	X2	X1	Y					
5	A	6	3	11					
6	B	5	2	9					
7	C	8	4	16					
8	D	7	3	12					
9									
10		OutsiD(X1)	Units(X2)	Constant					
11		2	1	-0.5					
12		2.236068	1.414214	3.570714					
13	coef of det	0.961538	1	#N/A					
14									

Notice how the coefficients for the independent variables are reversed. The coefficient for X1 (2) is displayed in cell B11, the coefficient for X2 (1) is displayed in cell C11, and the constant value (-0.5) is displayed in cell D11. The coefficient of determination is displayed in cell B13.

Always highlight 3 rows before you key your LINEST function. In the Excel output, the coefficient of determination will be the first cell in the third row.
Using row 11, you can construct a multiple regression equation to predict the tensile strength of the wire (Y)

Y = –0.5 + 2 (Outside D) + 1 (mol units)

4. In A15 to A17, key respectively, **Outside Diameter(X1)=, Molybdenum units(X2)=, Predicted Tensile strength(Y)=**

5. In D15, key **3.5**, in D16, key **6.4**, in D17, key **=D11+D15*B11+D16*C11**

This gives you the estimated tensile strength of 12.9. If you want to experiment to see what the predicted tensile strength would be for different values of the Outside Diameter and the Molybdenum units, you can key in other values for cells D15 and D16.

	A	B	C	D	E	F	G	H	I
3		Mol. Units	Outside D	TenStrength					
4	Piece	X2	X1	Y					
5	A	6	3	11					
6	B	5	2	9					
7	C	8	4	16					
8	D	7	3	12					
9									
10		OutsiD(X1)	Units(X2)	Constant					
11		2	1	-0.5					
12		2.236068	1.414214	3.570714					
13	coef of det	0.961538	1	#N/A					
14									
15	Outside Diameter(X1)=			3.5					
16	Molybdenum units(X2)=			6.4					
17	Predicted Tensil strength(Y)=			12.9					
18									

Use Excel's LINEST function to construct the multiple regression equation for the following problems, and use the equation to make predictions.

Practice Exercises taken from the textbook.

14-1. Suppose that the sales manager of a large automotive parts distributor wants to estimate as early as April, the total annual sales of a region. Based on regional sales, the total sales for the company can also be estimated. If, based on past experience, it is found that the April estimates of annual sales are reasonably accurate, then in future years the April forecast could be used to revise production schedules and maintain the correct inventory at the retail outlets.

Several factors appear to be related to sales, including the number of retail outlets in the region stocking the company's parts, the number of automobiles in the region registered as of April 1, and the total personal income for the first quarter of the year. A total of five independent variables were finally selected as being the most important (according to the sales manager). Then the data were gathered for a recent year. The total annual sales for the year for each region were also recorded. Note in the following table that for region 1 there were 1.139 retail outlets stocking the company's automotive parts, there were 9,270,000 registered automobiles in the region as of April 1, and sales for that year were $37,702,000. (Textbook Problem 14-16)

Annual Sales ($ millions) Y	Number of retail outlets, X1	Number automobiles registered (millions) X2	Personal income ($ billions) X3	Average age of automobiles (years) X4	Number of supervisors X5
37.702	1739	9.27	85.4	3.5	9.0
24.196	1221	5.86	60.7	5.0	5.0
32.055	1646	8.81	68.1	4.4	7.0
3.611	120	3.81	20.2	4.0	5.0
17.625	1096	10.31	33.8	3.5	7.0
45.919	2290	11.62	95.1	4.1	13.0
29.600	1687	8.96	69.3	4.1	15.0
8.114	241	6.28	16.3	5.9	11.0
20.116	649	7.77	34.9	5.5	16.0
12.994	1427	10.92	15.1	4.1	10.0

What are the predicted Annual sales for 1,946 retail outlets, 8.65 million registered automobiles, Personal income of 93.2 billion, average age of automobile of 4.8 years, and Number of supervisors 12?

HINT: On your worksheet, list Annual sales last and the independent variables beginning with X5. Be sure to highlight 3 rows and 6 columns before you type your LINEST function.

14-2. The administrator of a new paralegal program at Seagate Technical College wants to estimate the grade point average in the new program. He thought that high school GPA, the verbal score on the Scholastic Aptitude Test (SAT), and the mathematics score on the SAT would be good predictors of paralegal GPA. The data on nine students are: (Textbook Problem 14-17)

Student	High school GPA	SAT verbal	SAT math	Paralegal GPA
1	3.25	480	410	3.21
2	1.80	290	270	1.68
3	2.89	420	410	3.58
4	3.81	500	600	3.92
5	3.13	500	490	3.00
6	2.81	430	460	2.82
7	2.20	320	490	1.65
8	2.14	530	480	3.30
9	2.63	469	440	2.33

What is the predicted Paralegal GPA for a High school GPA of 3.53, a verbal SAT of 560, and a math SAT of 450?

HINT: On your worksheet, list Paralegal GPA last and the independent variables beginning with the math SAT. Be sure to highlight 3 rows and 4 columns before you type your LINEST function.

CHAPTER
15
NONPARAMETRIC METHODS: CHI-SQUARE APPLICATIONS

CHAPTER GOALS

After completing this chapter, you will be able to:

1. List the characteristics of the chi-square distribution along with some of its uses and limitations.

2. Use Excel to conduct a goodness-of-fit test of hypothesis involving the difference between a set of observed frequencies and a corresponding set of expected frequencies.

3. Use Excel to conduct a contingency table analysis, a test of hypothesis to determine whether two criteria of classification are related.

Introduction

Chapters 10 through 12 dealt with data that were at least interval-scale, such as weights, incomes, and ages. We conducted a number of tests of hypothesis about a population mean and two or more population means. For these tests it was assumed that the population was normal. This chapter deals with the **chi-square distribution**, hypothesis tests where the data does not need to be interval-scale, but could be nominal- or ordinal-scale, and where no assumptions are made about the shape of the parent population. This hypothesis test is called a **nonparametric test** or a **distribution-free test**.

Characteristics of the Chi-Square Distribution

*   The computed value of chi-square is always positive because the difference between f_o and f_e is squared, that is, $(f_o - f_e)^2$.

*   There is a family of chi-square distributions. There is a chi-square distribution for 1 degree of freedom, another for 2 degrees of freedom, another for 3 degrees of freedom, and so on. In this type of problem the number of degrees of freedom is determined by k-1, where k is the number of categories. Therefore, the shape of the chi-square distribution does not depend on the size of the sample. For example, if 300 employees of a school district were classified into one of three categories--support staff, teachers, and administration--there would be k-1 = 3–1=2 degrees of freedom.

*   The chi-square distribution is positively skewed. However, as the number of degrees of freedom increases the distribution begins to approximate the normal distribution.

Limitations of Chi-Square

If there is an unusually small expected frequency in a cell, chi-square (if applied) might result in an erroneous conclusion. This can happen because f_e appears in the denominator, and dividing by a very small number makes the quotient quite large! Two generally accepted rules regarding small cell frequencies are:

- If there are only two cells, the expected frequency in each cell should be 5 or more.

- For more than two cells, chi-square should not be applied if more than 20 percent of the f_e cells have expected frequencies less than 5.

Use the same five steps in hypothesis testing that were used in Chapters 10 through 12:

Steps in hypothesis testing:

1. **State the null and alternative hypothesis** using either formulas or words. The null hypothesis (H_o) is always the statement of no significant difference.

   The alternative hypothesis (H_1) is always the statement that there is a significant difference. When direction is stated it is a one-directional test (one-tailed). When direction is not stated it is a two-directional test (two-tailed).

2. **State the level of significance** or the probability that the null hypothesis is rejected when, in fact, it is true.

3. **State the statistical test** you will be using: the z test, t test, F test, chi square test, etc.

4. **Formulate a decision rule**. Using a picture or curve that estimates the distribution you are testing, show the critical value if you are performing a one-directional test or the upper and lower critical values if you are performing a two-directional test.

5. **Do it**. Show the formula you used and at least the major steps involved. State the results of the hypothesis test in terms of the question using complete sentences and examples.

Equal Expected Frequencies

In this chapter you will be working with the chi-square distribution. There is no worksheet that can be created that will fit all problems of a particular type. What follows are examples of different situations. You will need to modify the worksheets when doing other problems.

The formula for the test statistic of chi-square is $X^2 = \Sigma \left[\dfrac{(f_o - f_e)^2}{f_e} \right]$

This formula will be referred to as Chi_Sq.

f_o is an observed frequency in a particular situation. It will be referred to as fo.

f_e is an expected frequency in a particular situation. It will be referred to as fe.

You will also need the degrees of freedom for computing the critical value. Degrees of freedom will be referred to as df, the critical value will be referred to as Crit_Val.

The formula for degrees of freedom is df = k-1, where k is the number of categories or *cells*.

Example 1. The human resources director at Georgetown Paper, Inc is concerned about absenteeism. She decides to sample the company records to determine if absenteeism is distributed evenly throughout the six-day workweek. The hypotheses to be tested are: Ho: Absenteeism is evenly distributed throughout the work week. H_1: Absenteeism is not evenly distributed throughout the work week. The .01 level is to be used. The sample results are:

	Number absent
Monday	12
Tuesday	9
Wednesday	11
Thursday	10
Friday	9
Saturday	9

What does this indicate to the human resources director?

1. On a new worksheet, enter the data as shown.

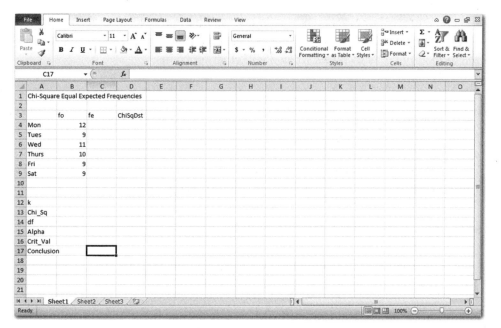

2. Highlight **A4:A16**. From the Home tab, in the Alignment group, select the Align Right icon.

3. Highlight **B3:D9**. From the Formulas tab, in the Defined Names group, select Create from Selection. Select <u>T</u>op Row. Click OK.

4. Highlight **A12:B16**. From the Formulas tab, in the Defined Names group, select Create from Selection. Select <u>L</u>eft Column. Click OK.

5. In B12, key =**COUNT(fo)**

This will count the number of categories and give you the value of k.

6. In B13, key =**SUM(ChiSqDst)**

This will sum all the cell contents that you calculate. It will temporarily read 0.

7. In B14, key =**k-1**

8. In B15, key **.01**

9. In B16, key =**CHIINV(Alpha, df)**

This computes the critical value.

10. In B17, key =**IF(Chi_Sq>Crit_Val, "Reject Ho", "Do Not Reject Ho")**

As you are keying, your cell contents for A12:B17 will look as shown below.

	A	B	C	D	E	F	G	H	I
12	k	=COUNT(fo)							
13	Chi_Sq	=SUM(ChiSqDst)							
14	df	=k-1							
15	Alpha	0.01							
16	Crit_Val	=CHIINV(Alpha, df)							
17	Conclusion	=IF(Chi_Sq>Crit_Val, "Reject Ho", "Do Not Reject Ho")							
18									

11. In C4, key =**AVERAGE(fo)**

This is the expected frequency (f_e). This value will be copied to cells C5:C9.

12. In D4, key =**(fo-fe)^2/fe**

This is the square of each difference divided by the expected frequency. This formula will be copied to cells D5:D9.

The cell contents of C4 and D4 will look as shown below.

	A	B	C	D	E	F	G	H	I
1	Chi-Square Equal Expected Frequencies								
2									
3		fo	fe	ChiSqDst					
4	Mon	12	=AVERAGE(fo)	=(fo-fe)^2/fe					
5	Tues	9							
6	Wed	11							
7	Thurs	10							
8	Fri	9							
9	Sat	9							
10									

13. Highlight **C4:D4**. Place the mouse arrow on the lower right handle of D4. It will look like a thick black plus sign. Click and drag from D4:D9. This copies both the expected frequency and the formula and completes the table . Also, the remaining cells are computed and the output is complete.

	A	B	C	D	E
1	Chi-Square Equal Expected Frequencies				
2					
3		fo	fe	ChiSqDst	
4	Mon	12	10	0.4	
5	Tues	9	10	0.1	
6	Wed	11	10	0.1	
7	Thurs	10	10	0	
8	Fri	9	10	0.1	
9	Sat	9	10	0.1	
10					
11					
12	k	6			
13	Chi_Sq	0.8			
14	df	5			
15	Alpha	0.01			
16	Crit_Val	15.08627			
17	Conclusion	Do Not Reject Ho			
18					

The results can now be interpreted.

Do not reject Ho. The computed value for chi-square falls in the acceptance range because .8 is less than the critical value of 15.08627. Absenteeism is distributed evenly throughout the week. The observed differences are due to sampling variation.

Save your file as **chi-sqeq**. Close your file.

Example 2. To use this worksheet to solve other problems not having six categories, you must first rekey the category data in columns A and B. If you have less than 6 categories, you need to clear any cells in rows below the last category. If you have more than 6 categories you must copy the formulas for the extra rows in columns C and D. In both instances you then need to use the Create from Selection command to rename columns B, C, and D using the new ranges. When you are asked if you would like to replace the existing definition, click on Yes. You may also need to key in a new value for Alpha.

In example 1, assume the business is also open on Sunday. You will modify the worksheet to include the extra category.

1. Open the file **chi-sqeq**.

2. In cells A10 and B10, key **Sun** and **13** respectively.

3. Highlight **C9:D9**. Drag the lower right handle of D9 to D10.

D10 reads #VALUE!, because cells B10 and C10 have no name.

4. Highlight **B3:D10**. Use the Create from Selection command to rename the cells. In each instance when you are asked if you would like to replace the existing definition, click on Yes. You will be asked 3 times.

As soon as you are finished redefining columns B, C, and D, the output changes to reflect the new data.

	A	B	C	D	E
1	Chi-Square Equal Expected Frequencies				
2					
3		fo	fe	ChiSqDst	
4	Mon	12	10.42857	0.236791	
5	Tues	9	10.42857	0.195695	
6	Wed	11	10.42857	0.031311	
7	Thurs	10	10.42857	0.017613	
8	Fri	9	10.42857	0.195695	
9	Sat	9	10.42857	0.195695	
10	Sun	13	10.42857	0.634051	
11					
12	k	7			
13	Chi_Sq	1.506849			
14	df	6			
15	Alpha	0.01			
16	Crit_Val	16.81189			
17	Conclusion	Do Not Reject Ho			
18					

If you wish, save the file as **chi-sq2**. Close your file.

Contingency Tables

You will create a worksheet to determine expected frequencies when observed frequencies are known. You will also create a table to compute chi-square. You will create a worksheet to solve the following problem.

Example 3. The director of advertising for the Carolina Sun Times, the largest newspaper in the Carolinas, is studying the relationship between the type of community in which a subscriber resides and the section of the newspaper he or she reads first. For a sample of readers, she collected the following sample information.

	National News	Sports	Comics
City	170	124	90
Suburb	120	112	100
Rural	130	90	88

At the .05 significance level, can we conclude there is a relationship between the type of community where the person resides and the section of the paper read first?

1. On a new worksheet, enter the data as shown below.

	A	B	C	D	E	F
1	Chi-Square Contingency Tables					
2						
3		Newspaper section				
4	Residence	Nat news	Sports	Comics	Total	
5	City					
6	Suburb					
7	Rural					
8	Total					GrnTot
9						

2. Highlight **A3:E8**. From the Home tab, in the Clipboard group select Copy.

3. Make A10 your active cell. From the Home tab, in the Clipboard group select Paste. Touch <Enter>.

4. Highlight **A10:E15**. From the Home tab, in the Clipboard group select Copy.

5. Make A17 your active cell. Home tab, in the Clipboard group select Paste. Touch <Enter>.

6. In cell D3, key **(Observed)**

7. In cell D10, key **(Expected)**

8. In cell D17, key **(Chi-Square Computations)**

9. In cells B5:D7, and cells A24:A27, enter the data as shown.

	A	B	C	D	E	F
1	Chi-Square Contingency Tables					
2						
3		Newspaper section		(Observed)		
4	Residence	Nat news	Sports	Comics	Total	
5	City	170	124	90		
6	Suburb	120	112	100		
7	Rural	130	90	88		
8	Total					GrnTot
9						
10		Newspaper section		(Expected)		
11	Residence	Nat news	Sports	Comics	Total	
12	City					
13	Suburb					
14	Rural					
15	Total					
16						
17		Newspaper section		(Chi-Square Computations)		
18	Residence	Nat news	Sports	Comics	Total	
19	City					
20	Suburb					
21	Rural					
22	Total					
23						
24	df					
25	Alpha					
26	Crit_Val					
27	Conclusion					
28						

10. In cell B26, key =**CHIINV(Alpha,df)**

11. In cell B27, key =**IF(Chi_Sq>Crit_Val, "Reject Ho", "Do Not Reject Ho")**

12. Highlight **A24:B26**. From the Formulas tab, in the Defined Names group, select Create from Selection. Select Left Column. Click on OK. If you are asked if you would like to replace the existing definition, click on Yes.

13. Highlight **B5:B7**. From the Home tab, in the Editing group, select the AutoSum button.

14. Make B8 your active cell. To copy, drag the lower right handle to cells C8:D8.

15. Highlight **B5:D5**. From the Home tab, in the Editing group select the AutoSum button.

16. Copy E5 into E6:E8.

17. Highlight **E8:F8**. Use the Create from Selection command to name the cell. Use the Right Column.

The completed, summed, Observed table should look as shown below.

	A	B	C	D	E	F
1	Chi-Square Contingency Tables					
2						
3		Newspaper section		(Observed)		
4	Residence	Nat news	Sports	Comics	Total	
5	City	170	124	90	384	
6	Suburb	120	112	100	332	
7	Rural	130	90	88	308	
8	Total	420	326	278	1024	GrnTot
9						

You will now compute the expected frequencies. For each cell the formula is
Expected frequency =(Row total)(Column total)/Grand total.

18. In cell B12, key **=$E5*B$8/GrnTot**

This formula multiplies the row total (E5) times the column total (B8) and divides by the Grand Total which we named GrnTot. The $ sign in the formula keeps the appropriate row or column constant when it is copied into another cell.

19. Make B12 your active cell. Copy the contents to B13:B14.

20. Highlight **B12:B14**. Drag the right handle of B14 to C14:D14.

21. Sum the contents of B12:B14. Copy B15 to C15:D15.

22. Sum the contents of B12:D12. Copy E12 to E13:E15.

The completed Expected table should look as shown below.

	A	B	C	D	E	F
10		Newspaper section		(Expected)		
11	Residence	Nat news	Sports	Comics	Total	
12	City	157.5	122.25	104.25	384	
13	Suburb	136.1719	105.6953	90.13281	332	
14	Rural	126.3281	98.05469	83.61719	308	
15	Total	420	326	278	1024	
16						

23. In Cell B19, key =**(B5-B12)^2/B12**

This formula subtracts the expected value from the observed value, squares the difference and divides by the expected value. The formula for chi-square is the sum of all the computed results.

24. Copy B19 to B20:B21.

25. Highlight **B19:B21**. Drag the right handle of B21 to C21:D21.

26. In E22, key =**SUM(B19:D21)**

27. In F22, key **Chi_Sq**

28. Highlight **E22:F22**. Use the Create from Selection command to name the cell. Use the Right Column.

The completed Chi-Square Computation table should look as shown below.

	A	B	C	D	E	F
17		Newspaper section		(Chi-Square Computations)		
18	Residence	Nat news	Sports	Comics	Total	
19	City	0.992063	0.025051	1.947842		
20	Suburb	1.920584	0.376072	1.080199		
21	Rural	0.106727	0.661651	0.229726		
22	Total				7.339916	Chi_Sq
23						

The last thing you will do is enter the values for degrees of freedom and Alpha. The degrees of freedom is df = (number of rows - 1)(number of columns - 1). Or (3-1)(3-1) = 4.

29. In B24, key **4**

30. In B25, key **.05**

This completes your total worksheet and gives the resulting output. The results can now be interpreted.

The null hypothesis is not rejected at the .05 level of significance. The computed value for chi-square, 7.339916 is less than the critical value of 9.487729. There is no relationship between the type of community where a person resides and the section of paper read first.

Save your file as **chi-sqcn**. Close your file.

	A	B	C	D	E	F
1	Chi-Square Contingency Tables					
2						
3		Newspaper section		(Observed)		
4	Residence	Nat news	Sports	Comics	Total	
5	City	170	124	90	384	
6	Suburb	120	112	100	332	
7	Rural	130	90	88	308	
8	Total	420	326	278	1024	GrnTot
9						
10		Newspaper section		(Expected)		
11	Residence	Nat news	Sports	Comics	Total	
12	City	157.5	122.25	104.25	384	
13	Suburb	136.1719	105.6953	90.13281	332	
14	Rural	126.3281	98.05469	83.61719	308	
15	Total	420	326	278	1024	
16						
17		Newspaper section		(Chi-Square Computations)		
18	Residence	Nat news	Sports	Comics	Total	
19	City	0.992063	0.025051	1.947842		
20	Suburb	1.920584	0.376072	1.080199		
21	Rural	0.106727	0.661651	0.229726		
22	Total				7.339916	Chi_Sq
23						
24	df	4				
25	Alpha	0.05				
26	Crit_Val	9.487729				
27	Conclusior	Do Not Reject Ho				
28						

Example 4. To use this worksheet to solve problems having other than 3 rows and 3 columns, you must modify the worksheet. If you insert rows and columns, (or delete rows and columns) **between** existing rows and columns, you will not have to re-compute the existing row and column sums. They will adjust automatically. If you insert rows or columns you will need to copy existing formulas to the inserted cells. You will also need to enter the new value for the degrees of freedom.

In example 3, assume the director wanted four levels of communities in her study. She also researched retirement communities. Her data for retirement communities was 125 National News, 97 Sports, and 112 Comics.

1. Open the file **chi-sqcn**.

2. Make A6 your active cell. From Home tab, in the Cells group, select the down arrow next to Insert. Select Insert Sheet Rows.

This inserts a blank row between two existing categories. As you key in the extra data you will notice that the totals in row 9 and column E will automatically change to reflect the current data.

3. In cell A5, key **Retirement**.

4. In cell A6, key **City**.

5. Make A14 your active cell. Insert a row.

6. Make A22 your active cell. Insert a row.

7. In cells A13 and A21, key **Retirement**.

8. In cells A14 and A22, key **City**.

9. In cells B6:D6, key **170**, **124**, and **90** respectively.

10. In cells B5:D5, key **125**, **97**, and **112**, respectively.

After these changes, your worksheet should look as shown on the next page.

	A	B	C	D	E	F
1	Chi-Square Contingency Tables					
2						
3		Newspaper section		(Observed)		
4	Residence	Nat news	Sports	Comics	Total	
5	Retirement	125	97	112	334	
6	City	170	124	90		
7	Suburb	120	112	100	332	
8	Rural	130	90	88	308	
9	Total	545	423	390	1358	GrnTot
10						
11		Newspaper section		(Expected)		
12	Residence	Nat news	Sports	Comics	Total	
13	Retirement	134.0427	104.0368	95.92047	334	
14	City					
15	Suburb	133.2401	103.4138	95.3461	332	
16	Rural	123.6082	95.93814	88.45361	308	
17	Total	390.891	303.3888	279.7202	974	
18						
19		Newspaper section		(Chi-Square Computations)		
20	Residence	Nat news	Sports	Comics	Total	
21	Retirement	0.610034	0.475955	2.695475		
22	City					
23	Suburb	1.315664	0.712884	0.22716		
24	Rural	0.330516	0.367545	0.002326		
25	Total				6.737559	Chi_Sq
26						
27	df	4				
28	Alpha	0.05				
29	Crit_Val	9.487729				
30	Conclusion	Do Not Reject Ho				

You now need to copy the formulas to the blank cells

    11.   Copy E5 to E6.

    12.   Highlight **B13:E13**. Drag the right handle of E13 to E14.

    13.   Highlight **B21:D21**. Drag the right handle of D21 to D22.

The only thing left to do is to put in a new value for the degrees of freedom. Since there are now 4 rows and 3 columns, the degrees of freedom is $(4-1)(3-1) = 6$.

    14.   In B27, key **6.**

The output in the worksheet has changed to reflect the changed data, shown on the next page.

	A	B	C	D	E	F
1	Chi-Square Contingency Tables					
2						
3		Newspaper section		(Observed)		
4	Residence	Nat news	Sports	Comics	Total	
5	Retirement	125	97	112	334	
6	City	170	124	90	384	
7	Suburb	120	112	100	332	
8	Rural	130	90	88	308	
9	Total	545	423	390	1358	GrnTot
10						
11		Newspaper section		(Expected)		
12	Residence	Nat news	Sports	Comics	Total	
13	Retirement	134.0427	104.0368	95.92047	334	
14	City	154.109	119.6112	110.2798	384	
15	Suburb	133.2401	103.4138	95.3461	332	
16	Rural	123.6082	95.93814	88.45361	308	
17	Total	545	423	390	1358	
18						
19		Newspaper section		(Chi-Square Computations)		
20	Residence	Nat news	Sports	Comics	Total	
21	Retirement	0.610034	0.475955	2.695475		
22	City	1.638609	0.161035	3.729343		
23	Suburb	1.315664	0.712884	0.22716		
24	Rural	0.330516	0.367545	0.002326		
25	Total				12.26655	Chi_Sq
26						
27	df	6				
28	Alpha	0.05				
29	Crit_Val	12.59159				
30	Conclusion	Do Not Reject Ho				

If you wish, save your file as **chi-sq4**. Close your file.

Practice Exercises taken from textbook.

In addition to showing your printout, state the results of the hypothesis test in terms of the question using complete sentences and examples.

15-1. A group of department store buyers viewed a new line of dresses and gave their opinions of them. The results were: (Textbook Problem 15-7) Hint: Use file **chi-sqeq** and key in changes.

Opinion	Frequency
Outstanding	47
Excellent	45
Very good	40
Good	39
Fair	35
Undesirable	34

Because the largest number (47) indicated the new line is outstanding, the head designer thinks that this is a mandate to go into mass production of the dresses. The head sweeper (who somehow became involved in this) believes that there is not a clear mandate and claims that the opinions are evenly distributed among the six categories. He further says that the slight differences among the various counts are probably due to chance. Test the null hypothesis that there is no significant difference among the opinions of the buyers. Test at the .01 level of risk. Follow a formal approach, that is, state the null hypothesis, the alternate hypothesis, and so on.

15-2. The safety director of Honda USA took samples at random from company records of minor work related accidents and classified them according to the time the time the accident took place. (Textbook Problem 15-8) Hint: Use file **chi-sqeq** and insert rows to accommodate changes. See Example 2.

Time	Number of accidents	Time	Number of accidents
8 up to 9 A.M.	6	1 up to 2 P.M.	7
9 up to 10 A.M.	6	2 up to 3 P.M.	8
10 up to 11 A.M.	20	3 up to 4 P.M.	19
11 up to 12 P.M.	8	4 up to 5 P.M.	6

Using the goodness of fit test and the .01 level of significance, determine whether or not the accidents are evenly distributed throughout the day.

15-3. A study regarding the relationship between age and the amount of pressure sales personnel feel in relation to their jobs revealed the following sample information. At the .01 significance level, is there a relationship between job pressure and age? (Textbook Problem 15-34) Hint: Use file **chi-sq4** and key in changes.

Degree of job pressure

Age (years)	Low	Medium	High
Less than 25	20	18	22
25 up to 40	50	46	44
40 up to 60	58	63	59
60 and older	34	43	43

15-4. A sample of employees at a large chemical plant was asked to indicate a preference for one of three pension plans. The results are given in the following table. Does it seem that there is a relationship between the pension plan selected and the job classification of the employee? Use the .01 significance level. (Textbook Problem 15-36) Hint: Use file **chi-sqcn** and key in changes.

Pension Plan

Job class	Plan A	Plan B	Plan C
Supervisor	10	13	29
Clerical	19	80	19
Labor	81	57	22

ISBN 978-0-07-741682-9
MHID 0-07-741682-1

EAN

9 780077 416829

90000

www.mhhe.com